Finding God
on the Indian Road

Finding God on the Indian Road

Exploring the Intersectionality Between Native American and Christian Spiritual Living

CHAD JOHNSON

WIPF & STOCK · Eugene, Oregon

FINDING GOD ON THE INDIAN ROAD
Exploring the Intersectionality Between Native American and Christian
Spiritual Living

Wipf & Stock
An Imprint of Wipf and Stock Publishers
199 W. 8th Ave., Suite 3
Eugene, OR 97401

www.wipfandstock.com

PAPERBACK ISBN: 978-1-6667-7188-6
HARDCOVER ISBN: 978-1-6667-7189-3
EBOOK ISBN: 978-1-6667-7190-9

09/13/23

I dedicate this project in honor of my Grandpa Dude. The Dude lived every single day of his life in the deepest and truest ways of what it means to be both Native American and a devout Christian.

Chickasha Poya!

Contents

Permissions

Acknowledgments

THIS PROJECT WOULD NOT be possible without the guidance, direction, and leadership of the following amazing people. The work we have been able to do together is monumental and life-changing.

Genie McKee

Dr. Ruben Habito

Rev. Dr. Hugo Magallanes

Rev. David Wilson

And to my *Ishki* (mother in Chickasaw) for teaching me all these years who I am and what it means to be Chickasaw.

FOOTPRINTS STILL WHISPERING IN THE WIND

The mountains appear as monuments,

Great is the Father who fashioned.

In the shadow, your voice,

speaks with the approach of dusk.

I will forever lift mine eyes,

As the stars in the clouds whisper.

My heart moves with the leaves,

Joy stirs the chords of love.

The river sings your praises,

talking rocks echo the refrain.

I sing with voices of the birds;

my song will glorify thee.

The rain quiets the murmurs,

as the gentle nodding flowers toll.

Though I walk in moccasins, my footsteps follow thee.[1]

~ Margie Testerman ~

1. Testerman, *Footprints Still Whispering*, 12.

Preface

As a citizen of the Chickasaw Nation and a Christian pastor for several years now, this project is near and dear to my heart to say the very least. The intersectionality between Native American spiritual practices and Christian spiritual practices was chosen as a research topic primarily due to my own life and experiences. I have been blessed to share each. As a Christian, I have seen and heard a trend happening in which traditional forms of spiritual living are leaving Christians both parched and hungry. The great divide that was created long ago between Native Americans and the Christian church on a spiritual front is a topic both disheartening and promising. There is a great deal of opportunity for these two worlds, once distant and separated, to come together and allow for a new expression of spiritual living to flourish. Much like what I have experienced in my own spiritual life as both a Christian and Native.

It is crucial to understand the vastness of the subjects being researched and discussed in this project. To begin with, the term "Native American" is a broad term that can, and often does, create more harm than it does good in its usage. If not careful, the trivialization that takes place when this term is used to cover the immense diversity and uniqueness of Native American tribes can be detrimental. The simple truth is, Native Americans are not alike, do not share the same practices, and are as unique in context and culture as Brazilians are from Mexicans. Of the 574 federally recognized tribes by the Bureau of Indian Affairs, each one is as unique as the other. This goes without saying many tribes have factions within the larger tribe with their own identity and cultural practices. To put it another way, the fry bread recipes are not all the same intertribally, and many Natives consider the correct way to make this sacred bread fightin' words. I will be using a few terms synonymously when referring to Native American peoples. Native Americans, Natives, Native peoples, Indigenous peoples, American Indians, or First American's are all terms I will use to name the Indigenous peoples of the United States. These people are the 574 registered Native American tribes and those who are unregistered and no longer in existence but were at one time.

The other important aspect to grasp regarding this work is the view of focus. To try and tackle a work that encapsulates the vastness and broadness of Native American cultures and spiritual practices would be a monumental task. The tribes in the East are far different than those in the West as well as those in the North and South. For that reason, this work will focus on those tribes with ancestral ties to lands in the southeastern region of the North American continent. Although many of these tribes now reside in Oklahoma due to the historic 1830 Native American Removal Act and other events, the ancestral lands of these tribes spread out across the southeastern area of the United States.

Researching this project took plenty of hands-on aspects such as spending time in Oklahoma where the majority of these tribes are still centrally located. Various cultural centers, libraries, museums, and historic buildings provided the foundation for research from the Native American view of the project. The other side of the project draws from personal experience as a pastor and a historical analysis of traditional and ancient forms of Christian spirituality. This was often paired with a social perspective of why there is a disconnect from the traditional praxis. A historical, social, cultural, theological, psychological approach gave way to a new way of living spiritually in connection with God.

Relocation for the Five Civilized Tribes brought about a drastically new context for many Native American people. The Seminole encountered arguably the most drastic change coming from their homelands in middle Florida to eastern Oklahoma. The Cherokee people sought new refuge in northeastern Oklahoma traveling through Tennessee and Missouri from their northern Georgia homelands. Similarly, the Creek people came from middle western Georgia where they settled in the middle eastern part of Oklahoma. The Choctaw and Chickasaw people from Mississippi, Chickasaw from the northern part and Choctaw from the central area, found a new home in southern Oklahoma. Not only were the territorial areas of these tribes now tragically smaller, but the landscape itself, which has a direct influence on social, cultural, and even spiritual aspects, was now radically different.

The title *Finding God on the Indian Road* is derived from language developed during the missionary efforts to "convert" and "redeem" the Native American people. Missionaries began to refer to their efforts and the evangelistic mission of converting Indian peoples as the Jesus Road. Although the Jesus Road has become a harbor of where Christianity and Native American spirituality live together, this was not always the case. Churches like Mt. Scott Kiowa United Methodist Church of the Oklahoma Indian Missionary Conference who claim one-hundred-plus years on the Indian Road are emblematic of what this book hopes to encourage in the larger Native American community. This "Jesus Road" is remembered for oppressing the culture, traditions, spiritual practices, and ways of life of Native American people to make them into the idyllic and colonized understanding and example of Christianity that predated first contact. The Jesus Road became an emblem of the widespread oppression and discrimination that took place in the name of God to change the ways of Native people to fit a more European image. For Europeans, the Jesus Road was the road to salvation; for Native Americans, it was the road to loss of identity and self. The Indian Road is the road that Native Americans took in denial of the Christian way. The Jesus Road perpetuated the mentality that removal of the Indian ways of life would open up the door for the Christian way of life to flourish. The reality is that missionaries, colonists, settlers, and early evangelists utterly missed the fact that God was very much alive and present on the Indian Road in ways unimaginable on the unholy redemption of the Jesus Road during that time. The title works to illustrate the fact that God was very much present on the Indian Road and in the lives of Indian people in the practices, customs, traditions, and ways of life that so many others worked diligently to dilute and ultimately eradicate. The title also stems from the conversion of Saul of Tarsus, later renamed Paul, on the Damascus Road. The story of Paul's conversion on the road to Damascus is one many Christians are familiar with and can orate to some degree. The story is first told in Acts 9:1–19 and retold by Paul in Acts 22:6–21 and Acts 26:12–18. Saul of Tarsus, a Pharisee in Jerusalem after the crucifixion and resurrection of Jesus Christ, swore to wipe out the new Christian church in its entirety, believing it to be blasphemy at the very least. As Saul journeyed on the road, a miraculous event took place where Paul was converted and began the journey toward the life dedicated ministry he would have that would influence many early Christian communities. Just as Paul had a conversion experience on the Damascus Road, it is the hope of this work that readers will have a conversion experience on the Indian Road. Many would argue that the oppressive acts of the Jesus Road held less Christian values and showed less Christlike ways than Native Americans demonstrated and lived by before first contact. To say God was found on the Indian Road, at the time, would be a contradiction and disrespectful statement according to the early missionaries and colonists. God was more present on the Indian Road than the Jesus Road of the time, and this is the starting place for the work at hand. As we endeavor on the Indian Road toward a deeper appreciation, understanding, and reverence for Native American people and our traditional ways, perhaps God's presence will be found in ways before thought unimaginable.

Introduction

I WILL NEVER FORGET the day that Ted came into my office asking to speak with me about his spiritual life and well-being. I remember being thrilled to be sought out in such a way regarding an area of Christian life I cherish and adore so strongly. As we met, Ted voiced his deep sense of longing to be connected with God, and yet, the overwhelming distance he felt at the same time. As we spoke, Ted was adamant that he just needed a few new practices to try, which he was sure would lead him back to God. Reluctantly, because I felt the issue was much deeper than what a few practices could mend, I provided several ideas that I assumed he had not previously tried. Several weeks later this same parishioner came back and asked to speak with me again. This time Ted voiced the same issue, as the suggested prescriptions did not work. After a second attempt of speaking to the possible deeper issues in his spiritual life, and again being deflected, I provided a few more practices to try at Ted's behest. Several weeks later I found myself sitting in the same office, with the same person, repeating the same conversation, and coming up with the same conclusion. Possibly a drastic misunderstanding of the phrase "if at first you don't succeed, try, try again" on the behalf of this parishioner who was present.

This experience in my ministry provides several different issues that are widely believed to be plaguing the twenty-first-century Christian church. First is the issue with Ted's lack of understanding of what constitutes a spiritual living and its vital role in the lives of Christian believers. As our discussions unfolded across the next several months, the identity crises this person was having and his inability to face his spirituality crisis came to light. Our discussions were able to reveal that this was the area to be addressed, and no matter how many practices he threw on top of this issue, it could not magically wave the problem away. It also allowed for a deeper discussion into what the role of spiritual disciplines/practices are in the life of faith. Many people misunderstand these practices as remedies, cures, or fix-all's. This approach often results in the person feeling more distant from God than they began with. A deeper understanding emerges when we see these practices as a means of God's grace that allow God's grace to flow in and through our lives as we grow to be more Christlike.

The second issue is with the high-speed, on-demand, constantly-new, and fresh world we live in. This world has created in the faith world a sense of constant desire and need for new and fresh. Where some part of this needs to be rejected, as it can easily create a lack of thankfulness and appreciation for that which God has provided, there is some part that must be embraced. No matter how hard we try, we have to accept that there will constantly be a part of us that wants new and fresh ways of experiencing God. This is not always a bad thing! As I have pastored, networked with other pastors, and studied this topic, it has become apparent the great need for a fresh and deeper way of experiencing a spiritual connection with God. Traditional practices of Christian spirituality are important and vital for faith formation and deeper connection with God, but there is a strong desire for fresh expressions that allow believers to find God in new and deeper ways. The more we can embrace finding God in all aspects of life, especially the unexpected places, the more we can hope to experience life in fuller connection with God, the great I Am.

The third issue can be seen in the difficulty I had in finding new practices for this parishioner, as Ted was very well versed in spiritual practices and disciplines. Because Ted was so well versed in spiritual practices, I had to become very creative in what I suggested and how I suggested going about these practices. What became clear was the reality that the flaw was not in the practice itself, but more in the fact that the practice felt "ancient, dusty, and outdated," as Ted so eloquently put it. Time and time again, when I suggested different practices, I would be met with Ted's frustration of having already attempted that particular practice in the past and the continued question: "Don't you have anything new I could try?" The truth is these ancient spiritual disciplines are time-tested and deeply powerful—a truth that has been revealed in the experience of the church over the ages. The issue lies more in their traditional feel in an ever-evolving world.

Several weeks later the same parishioner came back with the same problem, and I found myself frustrated and out of "prescriptions," as Ted referred to them. It then hit me that no matter how many practices I suggest, nothing was going to mend the deep separation this person felt from God until the deeper issues were addressed. It was time to stop letting Ted deflect from what I originally set out to speak about and get down to what was bothering him. As we sat in my office this time, Ted pleaded for me to simply suggest a few more practices that he felt would correct the issue, to which I asked if I could share a little from my own life. I began to speak about answering my call to ministry and how at that time I tried every spiritual practice in the book as I ran from God in what I like to call my "Jonah Routine." Ultimately, I had misunderstood what living spiritually is and lacked an understanding of these sacred acts as a means of grace and discipline. I was letting the high-speed, on-demand, fast-paced, new, and fresh mentality of the secular world invade my faith and the result was a lack of both holiness and wholeness. Eventually, I had to resolve that many of the traditional Christian spiritual practices felt outdated, out of touch, and out of context with my life and I was going to have to lean on other areas of my life to help remedy this problem.

It was at this point in my life that I began to lean deeply into my identity as a Native American, and it was at this point that everything changed. The day I began to let my heritage occupy my faith life was the day that my spiritual life began to transform. I stopped believing the historic lie that Native American spirituality and Christian spirituality could never mix. I began to see a new path emerging as I let my heritage and faith walk side by side, hand in hand. I began to understand that there was a deeper issue that these practices couldn't fix because that's not their intent or role. My struggles with my call to ministry could not, and would not, be easily remedied or mended with spiritual practices. As I stopped denying my heritage, my faith, and my calling, I began to find healing and wholeness in my life, which allowed me to live more deeply with God and experience all that the spiritual disciplines and practices had to offer. I also soon realized that I had to stop and practice simple living when it came to my faith. Simple living that is not held by the demands of the outside world. The fast-paced, on-demand, constantly-fresh, and new world we live in is both a curse and a cure that must be held in careful balance. To let this mentality be the driving force in my life would lead to a life that is constantly unsatisfied, unthankful, unappreciative, and unfulfilled. On the same note, to completely deny this mentality halts ingenuity, innovation, creativity, and creation. Therefore, these two aspects must be held in tension with each other. The traditions that exist and have been proven to be effective must be revered and honored without diluting or infecting their intent. The long-standing practices of Christian spiritual living must be deeply appreciated and valued for their ability as a means of God's amazing grace. With that being said, finding God in new and unexpected places is a practice that should never cease to exist. This drive allows the Holy Spirit to move in never-before-seen ways and impact people's lives in deeper ways as they seek to live in connection and communion with God.

Lastly, I began to understand that being a Native American and living in constant connection with *Chihowa* (God in Chickasaw) meant that I had at the ready an arsenal of fresh expressions of living spiritually that greatly aligned with many traditional Christian practices. In no way did these negate or replace traditional Christian practices that I and Christianity hold so dearly. Instead, it allowed for a deeper understanding and appreciation to emerge of spiritual living from a new perspective. My experience as a pastor has revealed a great need in the Christian church for a new and fresh expression, paired with a deeper understanding of spiritual living and connection with God. As a Christian believer, I have found myself wanting a new path to emerge that leads to living more deeply connected with God spiritually. As a Native American, I have felt trapped by the prevailing notions and misguided beliefs that Native American and Christian spirituality can never be intermixed. All of this together has allowed me to find a new path. A path of spiritual living that is both fresh and new, as well as deep and wide. A deeper appreciation of the intersectionality between Native American spirituality and Christian spirituality can work to bring healing and wholeness between two groups with a history of hurt and oppression. Additionally, exploration of the commonalities between the two will reveal a new and deeper way of living a spiritual life of connection with God. In essence, the words of Margie Testerman ring out in my heart and mind. Her poem *The Wind Still Whispers* is a testament to her faith and heritage. I invite us all to throw on our moccasins, because "though I walk in moccasins, my footsteps follow thee."[1]

1. Testerman, *Footprints Still Whispering*, 12.

I

Learning from the Path Already Trod

Martin Luther King Jr. is often referenced as having said, "If we are to go forward, we must go back and rediscover these precious values—that all reality hinges on moral foundations and that all reality has spiritual control."[1] It seems a wise place for beginning the work of exploring the intersectionality between Native American and Christian spirituality. This, unfortunately, is a troublesome topic and is a hurtful past that many do not encourage revisiting or delving into. The history between the Native American people and the Christian Church has a rocky and oppressive past that has left a permanent mark on both communities. For Native Americans, many feel their truest and deepest spiritual selves don't have and have never had a place within the Christian church. Richard Twiss shares,

> Several years ago, I attended some Native Christian meetings on a particular reservation. The camping area and meetings were adjacent to the central powwow grounds of their tribe. A number of the Christian Indians would not walk the several hundred yards to visit relatives or friends or even observe the powwow celebration because, in their view, Jesus had saved them out of "Egypt"; and they had no desire to return. They have

1. King, "Rediscovering Lost Values," para. 47.

been taught that many of their own cultural traditions were of the devil and should be avoided now that they were Christians. Sadly, this perspective among Christian Natives is not a rarity or exception, but for many years has been the norm.[2]

At the same time, the Christian community has found itself lacking the spiritual vibrancy that it could have had. This past has left a void between the two and has created space for certain beliefs and opinions to form that the two cannot and should not mix or complement the other. The historical precedents of an oppressive and harmful past have impacted the Native American and Christian communities to this day, and it is because of this reason that many have become complacent with simply letting things remain separate and void. The historical analysis of Native American and Christian spirituality before and after the European colonization of America, which began in 1492, signifies a dramatic shift in both the historical and spiritual landscapes. This marker point stands as a point of analysis for understanding the harmful colonialism that took place and its role in the spiritual world concerning Native Americans. The disturbing shift that history reveals is an oppressive religious endeavor that permanently subdued and harmed Native American spirituality.

BETTER WOULD IT HAVE BEEN

Joel W. Martin and Mark A. Nicholas write in their book, *Native Americans, Christianity, and the Reshaping of the American Religious Landscape,* about a young Cherokee man named David Brown who was asked to speak about Christian missions to Native peoples. "To drive home the damage done by Europeans in the New World, he invoked the life of North Americans before 1492, providing a prelapsarian portrait tinted in positive colors. 'They were once independent and happy . . . free from direful and destructive wars . . . in a more tranquil and prosperous state

2. Twiss, *One Church, Many Tribes,* 80.

previous to their acquaintance than at any subsequent period."[3] David Brown's statement that night to the gathered group of white Christians in Salem, Massachusetts, contested the widely accepted and naively formed image of Native Americans in calamitous need of spiritual renewal, awakening, and civilizing.[4] The harsh reality is that before colonization in 1492, Native Americans were considered by many far better off. The colonization of Europeans in the late fifteenth century brought about disastrous diseases that decimated entire tribes. Not to mention the avaricious desire for more land reconstructed the terrestrial balance of Indigenous peoples. Leaning again on the words of David Brown, who writes, "As things have been in America, for three hundred years, better would it have been, had the natives never seen the shadow of a white man."[5] Although a strong statement, there is certainly historical and practical support for such a profound claim. The historic analysis of Native American history in America, especially that involved with the colonization from the Christian church, reveals a past of oppression, segregation, close-mindedness, ignorance, and privilege that decimated Native American culture and spiritual practices, creating a divide still present to this day.

So, what was life like before that historic moment when Columbus first encountered America in 1492? To begin this historical endeavor, it must first be stated that this subject matter is plagued with deeply rooted harm and injustice towards Native American peoples and is, at its least, very complex and littered with contradictions. The difficulty lies in the fact that there is little to no historical record before 1492 of the American landscape. "Too often the story of Christian missions among Native Americans has tended toward one-dimensional renderings or particular methodological studies of events."[6] What is evident is that this pivotal event in history marked a significant transitional period in American history.

3. Martin and Nicholas, *Native Americans, Christianity*, 1.

4. Martin and Nicholas, *Native Americans, Christianity*, 2.

5. Martin and Nicholas, *Native Americans, Christianity*, 2.

6. Martin and Nicholas, *Native Americans, Christianity*, xi.

The gallant efforts of authors like Frederick E. Hoxie, Cameron B. Wesson, Charles C. Mann, and the historical endeavor of various tribes give a glimpse into the pre-colonization world of the late fifteenth century. Charles C. Mann, in his work *1491: New Revelations of the Americas Before Columbus*, asserts that historians like Eduardo Ladislao Holmberg often misunderstood and discredited the cultural and social advancement of Native American peoples. "Before Columbus, Holmberg believed, both the people and the land had no real history. Stated so badly, this notion—that the Indigenous peoples of Americas floated changelessly through the millennia until 1492—may seem ludicrous. But flaws in perspective often appear obvious only after they are pointed out. In this case, they took decades to rectify."[7] The focus of Mr. Mann's work highlights the cultural and social advancements of Native American civilizations before British colonization and Spanish Christian missionary work. Cameron B. Wesson concurs in his work in *The Oxford Handbook of American Indian History*, where he writes that the cultural landscape of North America before the colonization movement that began in 1492 was immensely larger and more complex than the European landscape. "North America was home to a greater level of cultural and linguistic diversity than Europe. When dawn broke over North America on October 12, 1492, an estimated five to ten mission people, speaking more than 300 distinct languages, lived on the continent."[8] He later concludes that "we can be certain that the pre-contact Native cultures of North America were far more diverse and complex than any of the theories archeologists have previously devised to understand them."[9] To Mr. Mann, Native Americans lived and operated with a sophisticated ecological, economical, sociological, spiritual, and diplomatic system that denounces early colonization presumptions of the need for enculturation and liberation. This can largely be seen in the commonly misunderstood and yet widely accepted concept of Thanksgiving. While yes, there were Native Americans

7. Mann, *1491: New Revelations*, 10.

8. Hoxie, *Oxford Handbook*, 22.

9. Hoxie, *Oxford Handbook*, 35.

and pilgrims and a large celebratory feast was involved, it was in no way the nostalgic celebration commonly taught in schools. Heather Hahn writes that "these settlers made war on their Indigenous neighbors, seizing their land, and selling captives into slavery."[10] The story is more complex than what is normally taught and is another example of the dark past Native Americans have endured and the constant whitewashing that sugar coats and alters these realities.

Mr. Mann further argues that a deep analysis of the way Native American peoples utilized resources and navigated the challenging terrain of uncolonized America is crucial evidence of the sophistication of the Native Americans during that period. In describing the Wampanoag home called a *wetu*, Mr. Mann states,

> In the *wetu*, wide strips of bark are clamped between arched inner and outer poles. Because the poles are flexible, bark layers can be sandwiched in or removed at will, depending on whether the householder wants to increase insulation during the winter or let in more air during the summer. In its elegant simplicity, the *wetu's* design would have pleased the most demanding modernist architect.[11]

The Choctaw people were especially in tune with utilizing the resources in a seasonal aspect. "For millennia, we spent our summers near rivers with their fish, shellfish, and plant resources. In the winter, we moved to the forests with their abundance of nuts, especially hickory, and wild game, such as deer."[12] The tribe also claims, "Our ancestors developed the knowledge to make all of the items necessary for an abundant life from the materials in their local environment. These everyday objects embodied beauty, tradition, and a connection with the land."[13] James Adair testifies to the advanced techniques Native Americans developed in fishing the territory. These techniques ranged from using long rails made with canes and hickory splinters that tapered to a point for

10. Hahn, "Making of Thanksgiving," para. 23.

11. Mann, *1491: New Revelations*, 46.

12. "600 Generations."

13. "Traditional Art."

trapping the fish to diving under rocks using their clothes wrapped around their arms and anticipating fish to bite their hands where they would then hoist them to the surface.[14] This testifies to the deep understanding of the terrain and context in which Native American people inhabited and how to utilize resources, not only for survival but to thrive and flourish. It also speaks to the great hunting abilities of Native Americans and the fact that game was very much a staple of their diet before the introduction of firearms. "Southeastern Indians used walnut hulls, buckeyes, and the roots of devil's shoestring to stun fish temporarily. A chemical in devil's shoestring is similar to rotenone, used today to rid ponds of unwanted fish. An Indian fish-killing served as a community event that mixed work, recreation, and sport with a fine meal."[15] Agriculture was instrumental in the lives of so many tribes, including the Choctaw. "When you burn the land as our ancestors did, you aren't burning it down. You're cleaning up the land. The fires are small, and you have to watch them. But they have a big effect. If you burn it right, everything starts looking better."[16]

Mr. Mann goes on to speak about the religious sophistication of Indigenous peoples of America and argues that "as a rule, Indians were theologically prepared for the existence of Europeans. In Choctaw lore, for example, the Creator breathed life into not one, but many primeval pairs of human beings scattered all over the earth. It could not have been surprising to Choctaw thinkers that the descendants of one pair should show up in the territory of another."[17] While Mr. Mann goes on to speak to the openness of Native Americans to the existence of Europeans, it articulates both the religious and intellectual complexity of Native Americans. The creation stories of Native American tribes are both unique and fascinating in their approach to narrating the creation of all things. The Choctaw have historically held specific oral traditions

---

14. Adair, *History of the American Indians*, 180.

15. "Fish Killing."

16. "Jerry Lowman."

17. Mann, *1491: New Revelations*, 165.

concerning the creation and the migration of Indigenous people across America.[18]

Not only were Native Americans far more advanced religiously/theologically and philosophically, but also sociologically. This extended both intertribally and within the tribe. Mr. Wesson claims, "Like that of all human societies, Native American daily life was grounded in a series of social relationships, beginning with the family."[19] In general Native American communities held in esteem their elders who acted as teachers and guides in the community for future generations. "Traditionally there is a special relationship between grandparents and grandchildren. Sometimes children go to live with grandparents for their earliest education, to be helpful, and to keep them company."[20] The Comanche held, and continues to hold, a very refined social structure that began with childhood.

> A Comanche child's greatest start in life is under the caring, watchful eyes of their mothers, grandmothers, sisters, and aunts. Historically the Comanche woman diligently handled all the home duties in life. Their hard work ensured the daily survival of their family, their relatives, and all members of their band. They were the backbone of Comanche's life. Our women shared extremely close bonds with one another. Our women were strong then and remain strong today.[21]

Similarly, in the Chickasaw Tribe, "elders and family helped educate us in the ways of our culture. Some of our lessons are told as stories. Both men and women are *nanna anoli* (storytellers). We also learned by the examples set by *sipokni alhiha* (tribal elders), and through song, music, and dance."[22] Vernon Bull Coming writes how he was raised by his grandparents who taught him the value of the Cheyenne language, the importance of respecting elders, and

18. "Our Creation Stories."

19. Hoxie, *Oxford Handbook*, 26.

20. "Taking up the Warpath."

21. "Comanche Women."

22. "Life Lesson."

the values of treating all persons with respect and dignity.[23] The rich and complex social structures within tribal daily life speak volumes to the advanced nature of Native Americans and the rich lives they lived before the English encounter.

From a diplomatic governmental perspective, Mr. Mann contributes that "what is certain is that both Hopi and Nermernuh were part of a network of exchange that had hummed with vitality since ancient times and had recently grown more intense with the arrival of horses, which sped up communication."[24] This can be seen in any tribe during these times as tribes depended on each other and coexisted quite harmoniously. This exemplifies a clear advancement sociologically and diplomatically. Mr. Wesson compliments this argument by saying, "Additionally, rather than being confined to a series of autonomous self-governing communities, as many as a million pre-contact Native Americans belonged to large, integrated, multi-community polities commonly referred to by archeologists as tribes and chiefdoms."[25] The Cheyenne similarly were "divided into ten bands. The Council of Forty-Four, composed of four chiefs from each band, plus four peace chiefs, led the tribe. The council met once a year for group decisions, with each band acting independently the rest of the year. There were also four warrior societies: the Elk Scrapers or Elk Soldiers, Bowstrings, Dogmen or Dog Soldiers, and the Foxes."[26] Mr. Wesson continues this claim as he illustrates the trade circuits found in the Plateau region and the various hubs of commerce in the area.[27]

Charles Mann also shares a time when he was privileged to hold a fabric fragment dating back roughly a thousand years in age. He describes the fabric as "carefully made: a wrap of fine cotton threads, ten or fifteen to the inch, crossed at half-inch intervals by paired weft threads in a basket-like pattern known as

23. "Taking up the Warpath."
24. Mann, *1491: New Revelations*, 123–24.
25. Hoxie, *Oxford Handbook*, 28.
26. "Cheyenne Leadership."
27. Hoxie, *Oxford Handbook*, 31.

'weft-twining.'"[28] He highlights the way Native Americans utilized both cotton and maize in profound ways before colonization and more technological advancements. This was particularly evident in Choctaw society that designated a cooking month. As maize was harvested, this time of abundance would be celebrated as every able-bodied person would gather in the large cooking ceremonies.[29] These not only were a time of celebration, which are still observed to this day as times of gathering, but were times of preparation for the difficult and harvestless winter months to come. "Indians used the plant resources around them for many purposes. In addition to being food sources, plants provided medicines, building materials, dyes, fibers, tools, weapons, and insect repellants."[30] The ingenuity and superiority of which Native American peoples utilized the resources around them to clothe, home, sustain, and advance their lives is remarkable and stands glaringly against the colonist-minded notions of being uncultured and uncivilized.

Charles Mann also argues that the historic evidence of counting and writing further strengthens the argument of the complexity of Native Americans and the sophistication these societies had before colonization. This can easily be seen in the various languages which derive from similar sources, systematic counting and numbering systems, as well as seasonal ways of keeping calendars. "The Chickasaw year, divided from the moon's cycles, had 13 months. Time was measured by the length of a day, the phases of the moon, and the changing of the seasons. *Hashi holhtina',* (notched stick calendar), was one method we used to keep track of time. We also used bundles of cane to mark the days. By marking time, battles could be synchronized across time and distance. Meetings could be accurately arranged far in advance."[31] The Kiowa also had an elaborate calendar that was pictorial based. Credited with making

28. Mann, *1491: New Revelations*, 197.
29. "Cooking Month."
30. "Useful Plants."
31. "Tracking Time."

the most elaborate pictorial calendars, they recorded both a summer and a winter season "count" for each year.[32]

Another area of pre-colonization ingenuity for Native Americans was the phenomenon of mound-building. These mounds held various important religious and social aspects and are seen as a sign of Indigenous peoples' ability to construct organized and elaborate monuments. "In the context of the village, the mound, visible everywhere, was as much a beacon as a medieval cathedral. As with Gothic churches, which had plazas for the outdoor performance of sacred mystery plays, the mounds had greens before them: ritual spaces for public use."[33] For the Choctaw people and many others of the southeastern region, "the tradition of mound-building dates back about 250 generations."[34] "Moundville, on the Black Warrior River in western Alabama, was one of our ancestor's greatest cities—a place where the forebears of the Choctaw, Chickasaw, and other peoples lived. We had lived in the area for centuries before our common ancestors began constructing the city's earthen mounds 900 to 950 years ago. Moundville became the political and military center of a network of villagers, with ruling families living atop larger mounds arranged around a central plaza."[35]

MOUND VISUAL[36]

32. "Pictorial Calendars."
33. Mann, *1491: New Revelations*, 295.
34. "Mound Building."
35. "People of the Mother Mound."
36. Choctaw Cultural Center, "Onchaba."

The *onchaba* mound in Chickasaw culture served various purposes. In the time of the woodland, about 1000 BC, these rounded, dome-shaped mounds were built as burial sites for important people in the tribe. At other times these mounds had flat tops, holding temples as well as residences for tribal leaders and elders.[37]

Life before 1492 was in many ways a time of peace, plenty, and brilliance. The strong ability to utilize resources and a deep and vibrant understanding of the contextual landscape reveal Native American peoples' ability to not only survive but flourish. An inept ability to survive in rugged terrain paired with an immensely advanced religious and social system shows a people, not in need but thriving. The intricate diplomacy that spanned from within tribal lines to intertribal relations, matched with a constant ingenuity in capitalizing on the resources at hand in creating both necessities and wants, as well as vast linguistic, written, and time-tracking systems, discloses the reality of a people blossoming for their time. As good as these times were, as rich as they have been revealed to be, they were no match for the tidal wave of change that bore a king's approval, held a pope's blessing, and was driven by hunger and pride that would change the world forever.

"TOOK BY FORCE"

Christopher Columbus wrote in a letter to Luis De Sant Angel announcing his discovery, "As soon as I arrived in the Indies, in the first island which I found, I took some of the natives by force, so that they might learn and might give me information of whatever there is in these parts. And so it was that they soon understood us, and we them, either by speech or by signs, and they have been very serviceable."[38] Although there is more to this letter and this simple quote does not illustrate the extent of the experience that Columbus writes about, it does reveal a glimpse into the narrative that would take place in this new interaction between the white

37. "Life Lesson."
38. Columbus, "Letter of Columbus," para. 8.

man and the Native peoples of newly discovered America. The alarming phrase used that still inflicts a painful sting to Native Americans today is "took by force." It is this simple yet complex phrase that illustrates the reality for Native Americans in a post-colonization world. The impending reality that fateful day as Columbus set foot on American soil and "took by force" the Natives to get what he wanted and needed set into motion an oppressive and harmful reality for Native people unimaginable. Many have attested to the reality of Native Christian conversion of the suffering that resulted from evangelization and indoctrination.[39] The truth is, Christian evangelism and indoctrination have taken by force by Native people and others for centuries and have subdued and suppressed inherent, ancient forms of spirituality in their wake. In essence, this taking by force is what has been deemed colonialism. Margaret Kohn and Kavita Reddy in their article, "Colonialism," define colonialism as "a practice of domination, which involves the subjugation of one people to another."[40] Just from this definition, it is ostensible that the actions and mindset of Columbus were of the colonialist mindset. One point of consideration that must also be addressed is the difference between colonialism and imperialism. Typically, these two terms are used synonymously or interchangeably, and this leads to overwhelming confusion regarding the terms and their respective perceptions. After careful consideration of the etymology, Mrs. Kohn and Mrs. Reddy conclude, "Thus, the term imperialism draws attention to the way that one country exercises power over another, whether through settlement, sovereignty, or indirect mechanisms of control."[41] This is dramatically different from the understanding and definition of colonialism, which is less about sovereign control and instead takes on a more domineering and oppressive tone. It is rightful to say that Columbus was not in the business of extending the empire so much as colonizing the area to be a reflection of British culture. From a historical perspective, colonialism has been a phenomenon that is far

---

39. Martin and Nicholas, *Native Americans, Christianity*, 35.

40. Kohn and Reddy, "Colonialism," para. 1.

41. Kohn and Reddy, "Colonialism," para. 1.

reaching and has been observed in many different cultures. "The ancient Greeks set up colonies as did the Romans, the Moors, and the Ottomans, to name just a few of the most famous examples. Colonialism, then, is not restricted to a specific time or place."[42] To properly address the harm of a colonialist mindset, a conversation about the Spanish conquest needs to take place.

The Spanish conquest of America was a movement that resulted in great debate from theological, political, and ethical viewpoints.[43] This debate was sparked primarily within religious circles with the said conversion and salvation at its heart. "Christian conversion was the interior analog and effective accomplice of more visible forms of domination and displacement of indigeneity, and in some ways, the more destructive form of assault against Native peoples, which continues even today."[44] The harms that have been conducted in the name of God are vast, and the distorted understanding of the mission of God through Jesus Christ by the power of the Holy Spirit to convert and save the non-Christians at the detriment to their existing spiritual understanding and connection only more deeply reveals this misunderstanding. This absurdity went as far as Pope Alexander VI issuing a bull (decree) titled *Inter Caetera* which gave consent and blessing to Spain and Portugal to colonize the Americas and the residing Native Americans as their subjects. The decree gave details that promoted the colonization, conversion, and even enslavement of Indigenous peoples with the understanding that "we make, appoint, and depute you and your said heirs and successors lords of them with full and free power, authority, and jurisdiction of every kind."[45] The Pope justified these actions by inciting that it was "by the authority of Almighty God conferred upon us in blessed Peter and of the vicarship of Jesus Christ, which we hold on earth."[46] The authority was given with a clear understanding of all of creation being given by God

---

42. Kohn and Reddy, "Colonialism," para. 4.

43. Kohn and Reddy, "Colonialism," para. 8.

44. Martin and Nicholas, *Native Americans, Christianity*, 3.

45. "AD 1493: The Pope," para. 2.

46. "AD 1493: The Pope," para. 2.

for the use and God's people. This colonial mindset gave way to the capture of Native lands, Native peoples, and Native ways of life that have yet to be recovered in many instances.

It must be said that simplistic notions of Native American Christians not being Christian before colonization is a fleeting concept in today's more spiritually, theologically, and generally mature society. However, that notion was not present during early colonization. "The Spanish conquistadors and colonists explicitly justified their activities in the Americas in terms of a religious mission to bring Christianity to the native peoples."[47] Although the topic of militant force is recorded to have been debated within Spanish conquerors, it was always justified in some form or fashion as a needed method for the greater good of God's will. Not only was harm done in the way of militant force used in the name of God, but it also came in the mindset of religious converters at the time. Ultimately, Europeans refused to see Native American people as human, civilized, spiritual, or equal as distrust, greed, and pride fueled the unjust and abusive era that was unfolding. "For the most part, the English were never able to bring themselves to believe that Indian generosity was sincere. It *had* to conceal some treachery: generosity must precede extortion."[48]

The landslide that came because of colonization has forever damaged and changed the religious and spiritual landscape between Native American people and the Christian church. The sixteenth century brought about an unprecedented time of change for Native Americans. The horror stories that unfolded as missional efforts took over the newfound land built tensions that collided into what is one of the largest, if not arguably the largest, genocidal massacres recorded in history. As colonies began to pop-up all along the East coast, so did the drastic influence of fur trading, tobacco, and disease. The by-product of these new wonders would be centuries of oppression and marginalization that would almost decimate Native American peoples altogether. Charles C. Mann writes in the sequel book, *1493: Uncovering the New World*

47. Martin and Nicholas, *Native Americans, Christianity*, 4.
48. Page, *In the Hands*, 161.

Columbus Created, that "by a quirk of biological history, pre-Columbian Americas had few domesticated animals; no cattle, horses, sheep, or goats graced its farmlands."[49] This introduction changed the landscape tremendously and allowed innovation to take place that was not before possible or imaginable. It highlights the theme of the time of two worlds colliding together. The more modernistic world of Europe is being thrust into contention with the more traditional and centuries-old world of Native Americans. The social, economic, political, and cultural changes that this collision brought about forever changed the Native American people. "From our travels and trade with other tribes, we learned of the first European outsiders and their reputation for exploiting Indians. We heard they brought *abika* (illness) and death, wiping out entire tribes. Our tribal leadership was prepared for the Spaniard's tactics."[50] The Chickasaw Tribe goes on to record that the December encounter with Spanish Explorer Hernando de Soto is an example of the tensions that built between new coming colonists and conquistadores with Native Americans. De Soto demanded women, children, and men be enslaved in the Spanish name, prompting an all-out attack from the Chickasaw people defending their people and way of life.[51] Where most people will find this story as another example of the violent, uncivilized, and savage misconception of Native American people, the reality is that these acts were not common and were highly fraught with internal and external conflict. General William S. Harvey is credited with saying, "I never knew an Indian chief to break his word. I have lived on this frontier fifty years and I have never yet known an instance in which war broke out with these tribes that the tribes were not in the right."[52] Pushmataha of the Choctaw people states, "We do not take up the warpath without a just cause and honest purpose."[53] Just one example, the drastic changes and disturbances

49. Mann, *1493: Uncovering*, 57.

50. "European Encounters."

51. "Deadly First Encounter."

52. Brill, *Custer, Black Kettle*, 1.

53. "Taking up the Warpath."

in Indian life during the sixteenth and seventeenth centuries are easily identifiable and reveal the annihilation of polities, forced removal, severe loss of life, and a shift in power dynamic fueled by pride and greed. "Many promises were made to us that sovereign rights to our *yaakni* (lands) would never be challenged. Bit by bit, settlers demanding more territory increased in number and influence within the states after the American Revolution."[54]

As European countries continued to prosper while Spain and Portugal suffered economically, great competition emerged between European countries for land in America as overseas power dynamics were at play.[55] "When European traders first arrived in our land, we had almost nothing in common with them. Unlike de Soto, they were here to stay, and against our better judgment, we learned to deal with them. Although the English and French traders competed for control of our land, they viewed with each other to be our allies."[56] At this point, the impact of colonialism had impacted Native American people in the Southeast, Southwest, and Northwest in profound ways. Trade had introduced new ways of living that weren't all beneficial and the power and greed of European colonists was a force to be reckoned with altogether.

As Native Americans entered the seventeenth century, the climate and context of America had changed so drastically that traditions, customs, and ways of life were now becoming as extinct as the tribes were being plagued with diseases and unable to recover. The new era ushered in new forms of survival that were counter to traditional beliefs and practices. Tribes looked to keep up with the expanding world around them as much as possible and found themselves using any means necessary at times. One example can be seen in the Osage people who used their geographic location to their advantage, controlling regional trade to the point of expansion. Savvy about the changing landscape due to the introduction of guns, the Osage capitalized on keeping weapons out of their enemies' hands and worked diligently to keep them in the hands

54. "Broken Promises."

55. Hoxie, *Oxford Handbook*, 28.

56. "Outsiders Arrive."

of their allies.[57] By 1750 an estimated 1.5 million British colonists lived in mainland North America, easily outnumbering any individual tribe.[58] As war erupted between the British and French in the mid-eighteenth century, Native Americans found themselves with conflicting motivations. Chickasaw leader Payamataha encouraged peace between the Native peoples and a joint effort against the British. Other tribes, however, sought individual gain and took the opportunity to attack British settlements that were smaller in number in the recent expansion.[59] Although the war left the English bruised and the French retreating, Native American people stood in the wake, hopeful for a future of prosperity for their people. Native Americans in the eighteenth century encountered evangelistic fervor in an unforgiving atmosphere that made it unbearable for any form of new or differing expression of Christianity that incorporated Native Americans' inherent spirituality to emerge.

By the early nineteenth century, most Native communities in the southern New England area had been incorporated into the Baptist movement.[60] The Indian Removal Act of 1830 was a detrimental blow to the hearts and souls of a people desperately trying to keep up with the massive change that had taken place over the last several centuries. At the end of a grueling set of eight years of the Revolutionary War, the new nation faced many problems and difficulties that included diplomatic relations with Native American peoples. Struggling to find an answer, a hasty piece of legislation emerged prompting the forced removal of Native Americans from their ancestral lands. "Not coincidentally, many Native Americans have maintained for some time that places, natural resources, and religious ideologies are all interconnected. Thus, the forced removal of many Native Americans from their ancestral homelands during the historic period represented challenges not only in negotiating and continuing relationships with new

57. Hoxie, *Oxford Handbook*, 63.

58. Hoxie, *Oxford Handbook*, 71.

59. Hoxie, *Oxford Handbook*, 71.

60. Martin and Nicholas, *Native Americans, Christianity*, 43.

homelands, but also in leaving behind vitally important elements of their religions and identities."[61] For so many Native Americans to this day, the often termed "Trail of Tears" that resulted from the Indian Removal Act is a tragedy not soon forgotten. Many Natives today have ancestors only a generation or two ago that were directly impacted and lived this nightmare. The US government reared its mighty head, and the result was the removal of upwards of one hundred thousand Native American people with a death toll too substantial for the record.[62]

"'Was this not the sacred burial ground of their fathers?' Tushpa remembered the elders saying. 'And had they not hunted, fished, and dwelt there always? They could not leave all on earth they possessed—home, land, aged parents, neighbors, friends—and march out into a wilderness penniless and helpless and expect to live!'"[63] The Choctaw story illuminates the pain, confusion, suffering, and fear Native Americans endured during the removal years. With tensions at an all-time high, Native American people felt more helpless than ever as they faced the growing US government. Leaders of various tribes fought in courtrooms to secure and retain as much land and identity for their people as possible. Others fought in more physical ways toward the same endeavor. Mildred Imach Cleghorn of the Apache Tribe says, "Geronimo surrendered because he didn't want the tribe to disappear from the face of the earth. If he had kept fighting, they would all have been killed. They spent 27 years in prison, and withstood all that, so the tribe would not disappear. Now I want to preserve all that's left."[64] Sadly, the US government wasn't done yet. With the removal act in place and being executed with resistance from various tribes, the government also installed the creation of Indian boarding schools, also known as Indian residential schools, to assimilate Native Americans into the emerging US fabric. It was at this stage that the greatest blows to Native Americans would begin to be handed out.

61. Hoxie, *Oxford Handbook*, 33.
62. Hoxie, *Oxford Handbook*, 94.
63. "Tushpa's Story."
64. "Preservation of Indian Cultures."

As if the removal wasn't horrific enough, the massacres that often accompanied the forced removal are events that still ripple with effects in the lives of Native Americans to this day. The expanding nation brought drastic changes that had impacts both internally and externally. As the Indians fought to protect their land and way of life, the United States Armed Forces under the command of Lieutenant Colonel George Armstrong Custer sought to end Indian raids by weakening their arsenal and destroying their morale at the Battle of Washita.[65] The acts at Sand Creek are just one of the many stories that still bring tears to the eyes of Native Americans over the injustices done to our people. On November 29, 1864, as Chief Black Kettle was pursuing and establishing peace treaties with US officials, Colonel J. M. Chivington and his troops brutally and unwaveringly attacked a village that was allegedly under the protection of the US Army. Although the village at Sand Creek is reported to have openly flown an American flag along with a white flag to demonstrate that the people were at peace, the troops were killed and mutilated, along with an estimated 150 Cheyenne and Arapaho men, women, and children. This event quickly became known as the Sand Creek Massacre and several retaliatory raids quickly ensued led by Cheyenne, Arapaho, and Lakota warriors who, along with Black Kettle, had survived the unjust and vicious attack. "Sand Creek and Washita were justified under the doctrine of manifest destiny by a country that was greedy and hungry for land. . . . The people of Kansas, the people of the Colorado Territory, wanted to see Indian titles extinguished in those territories. They wanted us removed from our hunting grounds, they wanted us to vanish, as the sun does every day at sunset. . . . This ground at Washita really represents the blood of our ancestors."[66] The sad truth is even after this brutal massacre, Black Kettle was willing to negotiate with the government, continually seeking peace.[67] These attacks were spurred by a central, biblical, and theological mindset found in Genesis to "be fruitful, and multiply, and replenish

65. Brill, *Custer, Black Kettle*, 94.

66. "Henrietta Mann."

67. "Peace Chief Black Kettle."

the earth, and subdue it: and have dominion over the fish of the sea, and over the fowl of the air, and over every living thing that moves upon the earth" (Gen 1:28 NRSV). The land did not belong to Native Americans in the mind of the settlers because they were not Christian and were not using the land to be fruitful and multiply. Thus, their removal was not only just, but it was necessary to the duty of every Christian person.[68] The doctrines of "manifest destiny," "discovery," and "evangelism of the savage" fueled these endeavors and gave a blessing to the massacre and slaughter of a people that had yet to even gain their personhood in the eyes of their new Anglo-Saxon neighbors.

Other treaties included the Treaty of Mobile, which provided food, military protection, and manufactured goods with Britain due to the skeptical relations with the French as they intentionally traded items infected with smallpox.[69] The wording of this treaty robbed the Choctaw of their land stating that the land was "given" instead of exchanged.[70] The Treaty of Fort Adams was the first Choctaw removal act, which the Choctaw believed would be the first and last time they gave up land to the US government. This treaty came fifteen years after Hopewell at a time where Choctaw leadership still strived for friendly relations.[71] This would drastically change as the US government continued to take advantage of the Choctaw people and many other Native American tribes. The Treaty of Dancing Rabbit Creek gave the Choctaw people three years to emigrate from their homelands to Indian Territory. While only two-thirds initially traveled this Trail of Tears, the rest eventually emigrated, usually in family groups.[72] The focus of the Choctaw leaders during this time was securing as many assets and securities for the Choctaw people as possible under the gruesome constraints of the removal acts. The Treaty of Doak's Stand was enacted due to continued pressure from settlers who greedily wanted

68. Roberts, *Massacre at Sand Creek*, 19.

69. "Treaty of Mobile Stand."

70. "Treaty of Mobile Stand."

71. "Treaty of Mobile Stand."

72. "Treaty of Dancing Rabbit."

Choctaw land. The lands being offered up were of the Caddo, Wichita, Comanche, and Kiowa while still being occupied by these tribes.[73]

"In 1883 the Indian religious crimes code attempted to strip us of our religious freedoms. The law banned our ceremonies and religious practices. Authorities confiscated or destroyed our sacred objects. . . . In response, we held many of our ceremonies, like the sun dance, in secret."[74] As the US government continued its endeavor towards assimilation, it ultimately began to decimate the religious and cultural identity of an already battered Native American people. Adeline Brown shares, "I got a whippin' for speaking Chickasaw the first year I went to school."[75] "In the late 1800s and early 1900s, the federal policy required that all Indian children learn English to prepare them for future American citizenship. The government removed many Indian children from their homes and placed them in boarding schools to learn English and Anglo-American culture. As a result, these children often lost their native languages."[76] Another primary target was the religious and spiritual identity that colonists never attempted to understand or appreciate in any way. "In the continuing effort to change our culture, our children were taken from their parents and placed in government, or Christian boarding schools."[77] One tribal elder gives his testimony of the Indian boarding school saying, "I can remember when I was very small, being taken away from my parents. We were not allowed to speak our language, and if we did, we were whipped."[78] By 1900, the once 10 to 40 million population had dwindled to roughly 250,000. Twelve entire tribes that once lived in Oklahoma are now entirely extinct. In an article by the United Methodist news service, UM News, titled *Pastor Reflects on Abuses at Indian Boarding Schools*, Jim Patterson interviews United

---

73. "Treaty of Doak's Stand."

74. "Oklahoma Indians."

75. Milligan, *Indian Way: Chickasaws*, 39.

76. "Language."

77. "Oklahoma Indians."

78. "Oklahoma Indians."

Methodist pastor Norman Mark, a Navajo and United Methodist pastor with a three-point charge in Colorado who attended four Indian boarding schools during his youth. Rev. Mark shares that while at these schools, "he witnessed beatings and students having their mouths washed with soap when they spoke their native language. There was also sexual abuse, a poor diet, and some students being forced to fight each other for the staff's entertainment."[79] Rev. Mark ended up at the school due to his mother being pressured into allowing him to be taken away by threats to cut off her monthly check from the government. Donald J. Berthrong speaks to this from a Cheyenne and Arapaho perspective, saying,

> "Every aspect of Cheyenne and Arapaho culture was under stress, and the old ways of life were changing: the Indian could no longer dress as he wanted or wear his hair as had the old warriors; Indian marriages were illegal (though still practiced); wood-frame house replaced the tipi; the children were in the missionary, government and public schools; Indians had to conform to the law of the white man. The Indian policy of the federal government did not change."[80]

"The theory of the schools, as articulated by Captain Richard H. Pratt, who founded the first Indian boarding school in Carlisle, Pennsylvania, was 'Kill the Indian, and Save the Man.'"[81] Sadly, many Christian denominations have histories establishing boarding schools during this era. Presently, acts of remembrance are in place as September 30 commonly celebrates Orange Shirt Day, a day that promotes awareness about the Indian residential school system still impacting Native American communities in the United States and Canada. Also known as National Day for Truth and Reconciliation, September 30 honors the children forced into these boarding schools, especially those who never returned home. Tink Tinker, a member of the Osage Nation and professor emeritus at Iliff School of Theology, adds, "Pure and simple, these were not

79. Patterson, "Pastor Reflects on Abuses," para. 4.

80. "Compilation of Everyday Scenes."

81. Patterson, "Pastor Reflects on Abuses," para. 7.

educational facilities," he said. "They were training Indian children for manual labor, just to serve their white superiors. . . . Graduates from the Carlisle school had to take an oath to profess that they were no longer Indian to get their diplomas."[82] As Rev. Mark states, "I will see to it that nothing like this ever happens to my grandchildren,"[83] words anyone can take to heart.

The complex and difficult history only serves as a reminder of the lack of equality and regard for life that the US government has had towards Native American peoples. "It wasn't until 1879 that Chief Standing Bear of the Ponca Tribe was able to convince judge Elmer S. Dundy to be considered an Indian is a 'person' within the meaning of habeas corpus after offering the words "this hand is not the color of yours, but if I pierce it, I shall feel pain. If you pierce your hand, you also feel pain. The blood that will flow from mine will be of the same color as yours. I am a man. The same God made us both."[84] While Native Americans were now seen as human beings in the eyes of the government, equality and justice were still foreign concepts. The issue of American Indian birthright citizenship wouldn't be settled until 1924 when the Indian Citizenship Act conferred citizenship on all American Indians. At the time, 125,000 of an estimated population of 300,000 American Indians weren't citizens.[85] The fight for personhood and citizenship was a long and strenuous battle that took a great amount of time learning and navigating a system blatantly advantageous to Native Americans' white counterparts. Reality is seen in the disheartening history of treaties and policies.

82. Patterson, "Pastor Reflects on Abuses," para. 8.
83. Patterson, "Pastor Reflects on Abuses," para. 3.
84. "Standing Bear Monument."
85. "Standing Bear Monument."

BROKEN PROMISES, UNHOLY COVENANTS, UNJUST COURTS

"From 1778–1867 the U.S. made 370 treaties with different Indian nations . . . by 1900 every treaty had been broken."[86] Of the most heart-wrenching injustices done to Native American people during the early years of US history were the many broken promises. The terms "treatise," "policy," "diplomacy," and "acts" are all hollow lies that our people have heard too many times before only to have every single one broken and twisted to benefit non-Native people. Many people are not aware of the true depth of the injustice that took place in the name of diplomacy and government. "N. Scott Momoday (Kiowa) calls language misunderstandings within treatise a 'confliction of language.' He says: 'Native people thought of treatise as bits of paper with this calligraphy, this print or writing on them, and that was new to them, strange. They did not understand that as a means of communication, as a representation of the word, as such. They dealt at the level of the human voice. The spoken word was everything to them.'"[87] The tradition of the Native Americans giving their word followed by communal smoking of the pipe was a sacred act that sent smoke to the Creator and signified that the agreement was good to everyone. As Walter Echo-Heart boldly claims, "It is painfully apparent that the Court needs to find some theory other than conquest, colonization, or racial superiority to justify its decisions. That change would entail a paradigm shift in American legal thinking similar to that which prompted the Court to overturn the legal bases for segregating America."[88] With the European counterparts, treaties were a means, "a vehicle for vindicating and rationalizing legal rights, particularly rights to take land or otherwise appropriated from Native occupants."[89] These agreements, which white men had no assurance they would keep, eventually broke altogether.

86. "Oklahoma Indians."
87. Harjo, *Nation to Nation*, 3.
88. Echo-Hawk, *In the Courts*, 7.
89. Harjo, *Nation to Nation*, 15.

To understand the true depth involved in the brokenness of treaties made with Native American people, it is first important to understand what they are and how they come into existence. Stephen L. Pevar cites a treaty between the US government and Indian tribe as "a contract between sovereign nations."[90] Where Europeans did recognize the sovereignty of Native American tribes as early as the sixteenth century, that recognition has not always held as firm when it came to upholding the promises made in these treaties.

"The U.S. Constitution authorizes the president, with the consent of two-thirds of the Senate, to enter into a treaty on behalf of the United States. The Constitution declares that a federal treaty, just like a federal statute, is 'the supreme law of the land.'"[91] It is a supreme law of the land that is often bent, broken, and manipulated to benefit non-Natives skilled and seasoned in navigating the parliamentarian-styled legal system. Bruce E. Johansen in *Enduring Legacies: Native American Treaties and Contemporary Controversies* highlights many key broken treaties including the treaty of 1778 with the Lenape Tribe and the Pennsylvanians that was broken only four years later as war broke out, resulting in the slaughtering of the Lenape people and the weakening of their numbers as settlers took their land.[92] The Hopewell Treaty of 1785 between Cherokee, Choctaw, and Cherokee Nations and the US establishing protection and peace was broken only a year later as land and peace were forfeited.[93] The Canandaigua Treaty with Mohawk, Cayuga, Onondaga, Oneida, Seneca, and Tuscarora Nations, which promised land and peace, was broken over several years.[94] The Treaty of Greenville between the Shawnee, Delaware, Ottawa, Ojibwa, and Potawatomi gave peace only to lead to the Battle of Fallen Timbers almost thirteen years later.[95] The Treaty

90. Pevans, *Rights of Indians and Tribes*, 45.

91. Pevans, *Rights of Indians and Tribes*, 45.

92. Johansen, *Enduring Legacies*, 83.

93. Johansen, *Enduring Legacies*, 11.

94. Johansen, *Enduring Legacies*, 44.

95. Johansen, *Enduring Legacies*, 253.

of Fort Wayne between the Delaware, Potawatomi, Miami, and Eel River Tribes and the US was broken two years later as William Henry Harrison led an attack on an innocent Native American camp at the Tippecanoe River.[96] Later, the Treaty of New Enchota would forever impact the Cherokee people as three years after being signed, the Cherokee found themselves being forcefully removed and left empty-handed after many broken promises.[97] Last but certainly not least was the Fort Laramie Treaty involving the Sioux, Dakota, Lakota, Nakota, and Arapaho people and the US government which was violated four years later as the Battle of Little Bighorn ensued putting an end to treaty-making altogether. Where the planning and nuances of legalities are present in the process of treaty-making, what is unmistakably clear is the utter and unabashed lack of respect, dignity, and equality towards Native American people at the time these and so many other treaties were enacted.

"Discovery of the New World shook the foundations of Old World jurisprudence and initiated a movement to establish a body of international law."[98] Mr. Deloria and Mr. Wilkins go on to argue in their book *Tribes, Treaties, and Constitutional Tribulations* that the unbalanced and disenfranchised legal system of today against Native Americans is primarily due to the precedents set during the earliest legal engagements between Indigenous Americans and their European adversaries. Walter R. Echo-Hawk wholeheartedly agrees in his book *In the Courts of the Conqueror: The 10 Worst Indian Law Cases Ever Decided* argues that the cases of *Johnson v. M'Intosh, Cherokee Nation v. Georgia, Connors v. the United States & Cheyenne Indians, Lone Wolf v. Hitchcock, United States v. Sandoval, In Re Adoption of John Doe v. Heim, Wana the Bear v. Community Construction, Employment Division v. Smith, Lying v. Northwest Indian Cemetery Association,* and *Tee-Hit-Ton Indians v. United States* are the most egregious law cases decided

---

96. Johansen, *Enduring Legacies*, 207.

97. Johansen, *Enduring Legacies*, 29.

98. Deloria and Wilkins, *Tribes, Treaties, and Constitutional Tribulations*, 3.

against Native American in US history. Mr. Echo-Hawk argues that since the case of *Johnson v. M'Intosh*, the US legal system is overtly slanted against Native American people. Over five hundred years, a culture formed pinning the legal system against Native Americans, forming a precedent that has yet to be rectified. These are the cases that introduced the colonial doctrines of discovery, conquest, guardianship, and religious intolerance into American lingo, law, and culture.[99] Mr. Echo-Hawk illustrates that the appalling and ignorant legal fictions used to determine legal questions and other settler statements include:

- *"Aboriginal land is vacant land.*

- *The Pope of the Catholic Church can give the Western Hemisphere to Spain.*

- *Royal charters empower colonists to settle Native territory as if they were the first human beings in the area.*

- *The discovery of North America by European explorers transfers legal title of Indian land to the United States.*

- *The discovery of North America by Europeans can be equated with the conquest of that continent.*

- *The normal rules of international law requiring conquerors to respect property rights in the lands they occupy do not apply in America because Indian tribes are too savage and warlike.*

- *Native land is wasteland or a savage wilderness that no one owns, uses, or wants and is available for the taking by colonists—therefore any aboriginal interests in the land are extinguished as soon as British subjects settle the area.*

- *Native peoples have no concept of property, do not claim any property rights or are incapable of owning land.*

- *Christians have the right to take land from non-Christians because heathens lack property rights.*

99. Echo-Hawk, *In the Courts*, 20.

- *Native lands are surplus lands. Native peoples cannot govern themselves—they need guardianship or tutelage for their good.*

- *Native peoples are racially inferior.*

- *Europeans can engage in just war against Native people if they do not submit to colonization."*[100]

These blatant and ludicrous justifications for the robbery and lack of humanity offered to Native Americans are testimony to the long history of injustice endured by Indigenous American peoples. In *Johnson v. M'Intosh*, Native Americans lost the legal title to America due to a shift in view from landowners to now tenants.[101] This meant that Native American occupancy was now subject to dispossession at US government discretion. In *Cherokee Nation v. Georgia*, Native Americans were stripped of political, human, and property rights only to be annihilated by the state as Indian tribes were seen as unable to hold an action in US courts.[102] Another notable case, *Connors v. the United States and Cheyenne Indians*, resulted in memorializing violence as a viable and acceptable part of Indian policy justifying the massacre and brutality inflicted on Native American people.[103] *Lone Wolf v. Hitchcock* was a blatant and outright example of a broken treaty by legitimizing majoritarian burdens on the Kiowa, Comanche, and Apache. The case of *United States v. Sandoval* gave way to guardianship where federal jurisdiction was imposed over Native Americans to the result of Native children being taken, withheld from their tribes and families in ways unimaginable to regular citizens.[104] This reality was only worsened with the case of *In Re Adoption of John Doe v. Heim*, where a Navajo grandfather fought to retain his blood relative failed in court as the US justice system showed an utter and blatant disregard for the role of extended families, Native social structures, cultural teachings, and cultural practices

100. Echo-Hawk, *In the Courts*, 44–48

101. Echo-Hawk, *In the Courts*, 83.

102. Echo-Hawk, *In the Courts*, 105.

103. Echo-Hawk, *In the Courts*, 158.

104. Echo-Hawk, *In the Courts*, 202.

via discriminatory and ethnocentric standards.[105] Not only were children taken, but as *Wana the Bear v. Community Construction* showed, the deceased were not immune to the injustices of the US government either. The desecration and removal of hundreds of buried Native Americans remains reveal the failure and unwillingness of lawmakers and courts to address, incorporate, and protect Indigenous peoples' interests, sacred burial sites, and practices.[106] Similarly, the Ponca people of Ponca City, Oklahoma, have historic graveyards that have been seized by the local government and turned into landfills. As we will see with *Employment Division v. Smith*, even religious freedoms have rarely been afforded to Native Americans. Fueled by eradicating Native culture from existence, the court ruled from a place lacking the insight to see the deep religious connections, paired with a stark intolerance of anything new spiritually.[107] Further, *Lying v. Northwest Indian Cemetery Association* proceeded to hold hostage Native American sacred land and furthered the lack of respect for Native American spirituality and religion.[108] Lastly, *Tee-Hit-Tons Indians v. the United States* not only took tribal land but proceeded to destroy the delicate habitat that supported and sustained a tribal way of life.[109]

For Mr. Echo-Hawk, the injustices seen in the slew of broken treaties and these ten historic cases and so many others present an era of fervent sadness and remorse as that of a miscarriage. Just as we take time to mourn the miscarriage, we appropriately should mourn our past injustices against Native Americans and prepare for a brighter and more hopeful future. This historical account should act as a sobering and awakening reminder of the injustice that has taken place. For Native peoples, it is a reminder of our deep history and the need to endure and remain strong as a new era emerges. For non-Native people, it hopefully acts as a brief account of the injustices that are often glazed over or sugarcoated in

---

105. Echo-Hawk, *In the Courts*, 223.

106. Echo-Hawk, *In the Courts*, 44–48

107. Echo-Hawk, *In the Courts*, 298.

108. Echo-Hawk, *In the Courts*, 355.

109. Echo-Hawk, *In the Courts*, 360.

history classes across the US. For both, it is a cautionary marker of the need for respect, reverence, appreciation, continued learning, and humbleness as an exploration into what treading the sacred and spiritual path can look like from a Native American and Christian perspective.

II

This Is Sacred Work

THE DEEP AND TRAGIC history with the Europeans, the newborn US government, and Native Americans is a tragic tale of oppression, discrimination, massacre, abuse, lack of humanity, and marginalization at its best. Walter Echo-Hawk goes as far as to parallel the removal of Native Americans with the actions of Nazi Germany and the Jewish people.

Walter Echo-Hawk in his work *In the Courts of the Conqueror: The 10 Worst Indian Law Cases Ever Decided* highlights the similarities between the actions of Nazi Germany and the US government's removal of the Cherokee people from Georgia from a legal standpoint. When speaking of the ideology for removal, Mr. Echo-Hawk notes that both centered on a foundational prejudice and superiority espoused by widespread propaganda and Senate resolutions.[1] He then moves to explain that it was law that was the preferred tool for singling out both Jewish people and Cherokee people circling around state laws used against the Cherokee and the "yellow armbands" and forced identification cards required of the Jewish people.[2] The target groups were then stripped of civil liberties by way of judicial restrictions against Indians to

1. Echo-Hawk, *In the Courts*, 315.
2. Echo-Hawk, *In the Courts*, 315.

press charges against white counterparts paralleled with forced removal of Jewish people from major political, educational, medicinal, governmental, and other areas of influence.[3] This then led to confiscation of property where the US government enacted the Act of 1830 where land was dispersed via lotteries, water rights seized, and gold/mineral rights confiscated which aligned with the Nazi's banning and rescinding of banking accounts and businesses.[4] Eventually this led to forced incarceration pending removal where Cherokee people were kept in stockades prior to the forced removal of the 1830 Removal Act and Jewish people were held in ghettos and travel rights restricted.[5] The overwhelming parallels between these two horrific times in history only reveal the deep evil and hate that motivated the subjugation of the Native American and Jewish people.

This analysis draws attention to the level of injustice inflicted on Native Americans and the trauma that has resulted from this injustice. As attention is now turned from the past to the future, a cautionary note must be made. For true healing and wholeness work to take place within and with Native American communities, a sense of past must influence the present and future at the same time. As Richard Twiss writes, "For us First Nation people, following Creator-Jesus within our Indigenous cultural ways without submitting to the hegemonic cultural assumptions of today's conservative evangelicals is tough. I am reminded weekly of these neocolonial and ignorant assumptions as they show up on the radar of my life."[6] Although the past is only a voice of reason and guidance for us on this walk of life, it finds its greatest strength when it is embraced in the present and allowed to determine our futures. As the ancestors' voices are heard whispering in the wind, they cry out for a different time of equality and respect for one another. As historic Ponca chief Standing Bear advised in his noble question for humanity for Native peoples, "this hand is not the

3. Echo-Hawk, *In the Courts*, 315.

4. Echo-Hawk, *In the Courts*, 315.

5. Echo-Hawk, *In the Courts*, 315.

6. Twiss, *Rescuing the Gospel*, 17.

color of yours, but if I pierce it, I shall feel pain. If you pierce your hand, you also feel pain. The blood that will flow from mine will be of the same color as yours. I am a man. The same God made us both."[7] It is when these words can truly take root in the hearts of all people that racism, injustice, and oppression will cease to exist as love grows and equality flourishes. The work the rest of this project has before it must be seen as sacred work, holy work. It is a work that cannot and should not be taken lightly and demands to be approached with respect, reverence, and gratitude for its sacredness to remain intact. To begin to explore the intersectionality between Native American and Christian practices, a clear understanding must form of what is appropriate and, more importantly, what is inappropriate. As a wise and beloved Chickasaw man once said, "I may not be able to tell you how to do something right, but I can sure tell you how to do it wrong." These wise words lend to the voice of the past, who begs us to lend our ears that how to do things inappropriately has been shown, and now is the time to do things in a good and right way. A sacred and holy way, a way of love and respect.

EVERYTHING NATIVE

One of the most harmful and stereotypical prevailing mindsets concerning Native Americans is the naïve interpretation that all Native American tribes are the same. This broad and inaccurate way of thinking only serves to further condescend Native American peoples, as it utterly negates the historic context of various tribes and lumps together the richly diverse and vast spiritual, cultural, political, and social uniqueness of individual tribes. Just as the Removal Act worked to isolate Native peoples in the Oklahoma territory, this minimalistic mindset works in the same way of negating the historical contexts of tribes while undermining the profusion of uniqueness intertribally.

7. "Standing Bear Monument."

The tribes of Oklahoma quickly became more acquainted as our people filled the state of Oklahoma. Presently there are thirty-eight federally recognized tribes, thirty-nine including the Uche tribe, which is tribally recognized but not federally recognized.

To truly appreciate the various tribes, a close look must be taken of them individually. The shared customs, traditions, and ways of life are vast, but far greater are the nuances that differ from tribe to tribe. As mentioned before, this work will focus on the southeastern tribes of continental America primarily relocated to Oklahoma.

A substantial grouping of these tribes is of those titled and considered the Five Civilized Tribes. These tribes include the Chickasaw, Choctaw, Cherokee, Creek, and Seminole Tribes. "The term 'Five Civilized Tribes' came into use during the mid-nineteenth century to refer to the Cherokee, Choctaw, Chickasaw, Creek, and Seminole nations. Although these Indian tribes had various cultural, political, and economic connections before removal in the 1820s and 1830s, the phrase was most widely used in Indian Territory and Oklahoma."[8] This term in the present conversation is both contentious and refrained from being included in academic literature. "The word 'civilized' was used by whites to refer to the Five tribes who, during the 18th and early 19th centuries, actively integrated Anglo-American customs into their own cultures."[9] This is primarily believed to be the only choice many tribes had to survive the turbulent and divisive times they faced. "'Adaption and incorporation of aspects of white culture' was a tactic employed by the Five Nations peoples to resist removal from their lands."[10] The reality is that this was simply another means of grouping Native peoples together in order to box out the uniqueness and vibrancy of the different tribes. "Some members have declared that grouping the different peoples under this level is effectively another form of colonization and control by white society."[11] For many, the term

8. "The Five CIVILIZED Tribes."
9. "The Five CIVILIZED Tribes."
10. "The Five CIVILIZED Tribes."
11. "The Five CIVILIZED Tribes."

"civilized" is demeaning and carries the heavy implications of the "savage nature" of tribes before European contact. This mentality is prevalent both historically and now. Stepping beyond this settler mentality begins by appreciating tribes individually and uniquely.

Although only a few of the Oklahoma tribes will be included in this section, there is an entire realm of learning and studying to be done concerning the tribes of Oklahoma and even farther tribes across North America. The tribes explored in this section serve as a reflection of the uniqueness of Native American tribes and the vastness of their depth of spirituality amongst many other things. One of the most common and widely known tribes is the Apache. The Apache Tribe are a fitting example of the commonly misunderstood and rarely known fact that within tribes there are sometimes factions, clans, or subgroups that exist. Of the Apache tribe's subgroups, the Fort Sill Apache and the Plains Apache are the most well-known. The name Apache comes from the Zuni word *apachu,* meaning "enemy" or "not of Athapaskan."[12] The tribe centers now in Anadarko, Oklahoma, which is in the southwestern part of the state. The tribe is 1,800 members strong with an enrollment blood degree requirement of one-eighth and descent from an original allottee.[13] From a linguistic standpoint, Apache is believed to share roots with Athapaskan-speaking peoples and have close connections with the Kiowa and Pawnee people.[14] Early life for Apache included small family-based camps or bands where women tended to the garden and home life while the men of the tribe hunted.[15] This is a common thread that will be seen throughout many tribes, although tribal governments will have differences concerning women from tribe to tribe. Dancing is a significant spiritual and sacred act that often includes the various societies of the tribe that are broken down based on age and even invitation. "Among the Apaches, a young girl's entry into adolescence is the most important community ceremony. During the Sunrise

12. Clark, *Indian Tribes of Oklahoma,* 27.
13. Clark, *Indian Tribes of Oklahoma,* 28.
14. Clark, *Indian Tribes of Oklahoma,* 29.
15. Clark, *Indian Tribes of Oklahoma,* 29.

Ceremony, the girl is called 'White Painted Woman' and is the center of attention for the whole community. Everyone looks forward to several days of feasting, dancing, and certain rituals."[16] As with many tribes, the Spanish horse transformed the bison hunters into nomads who were now able to cover more ground and organize better strategies.[17] Apache dwelled in tipis, which acted as homes as well as sacred gathering places for ceremonial singing and dancing, as well as the use of the sacred pipe.[18] Like any other tribe, disease, treaties, and newly available resources rattled the foundation of the tribe in more ways than one. Similarly, the Fort Sill Apache derive their name from the confinement in the twentieth century and their dedication to their leader Geronimo.[19] Today's Fort Sill Apache are the descendants of the Chiricahua Apache Tribe, whose original region was in eastern Arizona and western New Mexico along the United States border with Mexico.[20] The Chiricahua share a linguistic heritage with the Chippewa and Athapaskan peoples.[21] Where the Plains Apache were more patrilineal based, the Chiricahua lived in family-based bands based on matrilineal descendance.[22] The Chiricahua is one of the most feared Native American groups to ever walk the earth. Their ruthlessness and constant warfare depleted their numbers as they constantly rivaled the Mexican people.[23] The Fort Sill Apache share with so many others the heartbreaking history of Indian schools where roughly one-third of their children sent to Carlisle Indian School in Pennsylvania tragically died.[24] Many traditional Apache ceremonies are still observed, except for the girl's puberty ceremony. The most known Apache ceremony is of the Apache fire dancers, whose

16. "Na'II'ES Sunrise Ceremony."

17. Clark, *Indian Tribes of Oklahoma*, 29.

18. Clark, *Indian Tribes of Oklahoma*, 29.

19. Clark, *Indian Tribes of Oklahoma*, 151.

20. Clark, *Indian Tribes of Oklahoma*, 151.

21. Clark, *Indian Tribes of Oklahoma*, 151.

22. Clark, *Indian Tribes of Oklahoma*, 152.

23. Clark, *Indian Tribes of Oklahoma*, 152.

24. Clark, *Indian Tribes of Oklahoma*, 154.

nighttime dance evokes the movements of the mountain spirits in the story the dance tells. This dance is exceptionally unique in every aspect from the regalia worn and the steps and patterns of the dance to the drums playing and singing. The tribe also celebrates the tradition of the tribal princess, where traditional regalia is worn.

Many believe the name Arapaho comes from the Pawnee word *Rara-pihu-ru,* meaning "one who trades,"[25] although the Crow people often referred to the Arapaho as ones who had too many tattoos, "many tattoo marks."[26] Linguistically the Arapaho are related to the Cheyenne people and are often referred to as one tribe, the Cheyenne-Arapaho Tribes. "Today, the Southern Cheyenne and Southern Arapaho are federally recognized as one tribe, 'the Cheyenne and Arapaho Tribes of Oklahoma,' a reference that distinguishes them from their respective northern divisions in Wyoming and Montana. The tribal government, headed by a governor, is headquartered in Concho, Oklahoma."[27] The Arapaho creation story centers on four primeval worlds and a Flat Pipe Person who floated on the water-covered earth until the Pipe Person was given power and all things came into being.[28] While the Sun Dance was banned, several members visited the Paiute Ghost Dance and brought it back to which Sitting Bull established seven leaders to go out and spread the dance within the tribe.[29] Later the Arapaho people were introduced to the Peyote ceremony. Amongst the traditions of the Arapaho are social dances at powwows to aid members and veterans in need. The Arapaho people continue to be involved with Flat Pipe rituals in Wyoming and the Offering Lodge, also known as the Arapaho Sun Dance, and many other rituals practiced in present-day Oklahoma.[30] "Social dances were important to Cheyenne's way of life while on the

25. Clark, *Indian Tribes of Oklahoma,* 33.

26. Clark, *Indian Tribes of Oklahoma,* 33.

27. "Cheyenne and Arapaho Tribes."

28. Clark, *Indian Tribes of Oklahoma,* 35.

29. Clark, *Indian Tribes of Oklahoma,* 40.

30. Clark, *Indian Tribes of Oklahoma,* 40.

reservation. It was their connection to their cultural traditions and their ancestors. Every dance is associated with a ceremony such as the Scalp Dance, Sun Dance, and Round Dance."[31] Arapaho have unique art, beadwork, and design motifs in their crafts.

The Cherokee people are another widely known and commonly referenced Native American tribe due to their successful economic developments that have served as a model for other tribes. The name Cherokee originated from the *Tsa-La-Gi* in Sequoyah language meaning 'principal people,' which was eventually translated to Portuguese, to French, and eventually to English as the word Cherokee.[32] Cherokee is viewed as an Iroquoian-based language with two of the six original dialects remaining.[33] Historically the Cherokee people dwelled in southwestern North Carolina, southeastern Tennessee, edges of western South Carolina, northern Georgia, and northeastern Alabama areas of the US before relocation forced them to the Tahlequah area in northeastern Oklahoma. In the Cherokee origin story, the earth was covered with water and the heavens where the animals resided became crowded. After a council of the animals, the water spider dove to the bottom of the ocean and brought up mud, creating earth, and the great buzzard was able to swoop over the earth, creating valleys in the earth, giving a home to the Cherokee people.[34] Language is the center and fundamental aspect of every Indian tribe's culture and traditions.[35] "Brothers, the talk of our forefathers has been spoken and you have listened to it."[36] The Cherokee clan affiliation was matrilineal and women of each clan chose their council leaders who had the right and ability to intervene in men's affairs when deemed necessary.[37] For the Cherokee, several ritual grounds center their spiritual practices. These celebrations and practices

31. "Dances."

32. Clark, *Indian Tribes of Oklahoma*, 61.

33. Clark, *Indian Tribes of Oklahoma*, 63.

34. Clark, *Indian Tribes of Oklahoma*, 63.

35. "Language."

36. "Language."

37. Clark, *Indian Tribes of Oklahoma*, 64.

include large feasts, dancing (sometimes through the night), Green Corn ceremonies, as well as Christian-based ceremonies that incorporate language into their services.[38] The Green Corn ceremony is a ritual where tribal members give thanks and celebrate the new year. There is a time for fasting, stickball playing, dancing, and feasting.[39] Celebrated in June or early July, its elements are still practiced by some Creek, Seminole, Euchee, Cherokee, Caddo, Choctaw, Chickasaw, Delaware, Ottawa, Quapaw, Seneca Cayuga, Pawnee, Keetoowah, Thlopthlocco, and Alabama-Quassarte.[40]

The Chickasaw (or traditionally spoken *Chickasha*, meaning "he who walks ahead") Tribe centered in Tishomingo, Oklahoma, is widely considered kin to the Choctaw people.[41] This can primarily be seen in the very similar language base called Western Muskogean, where the written language of Chickasaw and Choctaw are identical.[42] The Chickasaw people's ancestral lands were the Mississippi, Alabama, and Tennessee regions of the US before being relocated to the Ada area of Oklahoma in the south-central area.[43] "While certain aspects of our culture are similar to other tribes of the Southeast, we are distinctly Chickasaw. We developed our own rules for living cooperatively. Our people share cultural values, ceremonies, language, and common ancestry that keep us together as a tribe."[44] Although our tribe is smaller in number compared to others, we have maintained our independence and security while protecting our people and territories earning us the *kano poyaka* (reputation) of feared warriors and wise negotiators.[45] "In the Chickasaw religion, everything in the universe had a religious purpose or significance. They kept a lunar calendar and held celebrations at the beginning of each new full moon. They had a concept

38. Clark, *Indian Tribes of Oklahoma*, 73.

39. "Green Corn Ceremony."

40. "Language."

41. Clark, *Indian Tribes of Oklahoma*, 93.

42. Clark, *Indian Tribes of Oklahoma*, 95.

43. "Chickasaw Nation."

44. "Uniquely Chickasaw."

45. "We Are Chickasaw."

of 'heaven' and 'hell,' and religion also had medicinal purposes."[46] Historically, Chickasaw people have resided in towns dominated by matrilineal affiliation with each clan having a chief (*minko*) with two major divisions between the Impsaktcas and the Intcuk-walipas.[47] These clans were matrilineal, and the traditional government was matriarchal where chiefs were elected.[48] The Chickasaw people have a deep heritage of traditional songs and Stomp Dances as well as an avid stickball team. "Singing our traditional songs and shell shaking is an important link to our past. The *nani kallo hilha* (Garfish Dance) is a uniquely Chickasaw dance that we continue to practice today. It honors the garfish and mimics the movements of the gar in the water."[49] Chickasaw people live by a motto of being "unconquered and unconquerable" as our tribe has remained strong and resilient through unimaginably difficult times. Another sacred aspect to the Chickasaw is the dishes of *pishofa* (pork and cracked corn), *tuchie shafut puska* (gritted corn), and *tosher* (poke greens). Gathering together is crucial for Chickasaw people, whether it be family reunions, church meetings, senior sites, tribal meetings, or annual festivals.[50] The Chickasaw people live by the saying "Chickashsha poya: We are the Chickasaw people. We are still singing, dancing, and living Indian lives."[51] As Kelley Lunsford states, "Being Chickasaw means being part of an extended family. It's incredibly special."[52]

Widely believed to be kin to the Chickasaw people, the Choctaw derive their name from what many believe to be the Muscogee (Creek) word *cate*, meaning "red.[53] Linguistically the Choctaw speak the Western Muskhogean language that is closely associated with the Chickasaw language. The language of the Choctaw people

46. "Chickasaw Lineage."
47. Clark, *Indian Tribes of Oklahoma*, 95.
48. "Chickasaw Lineage."
49. "Nunna Momat Chicashsha."
50. "Chickashsha alhiha ittafamma."
51. "Chickashsha alhiha ittafamma."
52. "Chicashsha chiyama chikanoma."
53. Clark, *Indian Tribes of Oklahoma*, 107.

is a deeply spiritual and important custom to their people. "I see good things to come in the future. Choctaws used to be ashamed. Now Choctaws are not ashamed. They want to learn and speak the language. They will move forward in strength."[54] The original land of the Choctaw people was the Alabama and Mississippi regions of the US before being relocated to the Durant area of southeastern Oklahoma. The Choctaw have traditionally lived in *iksas* ("clans" or "churches") that were matrilineally based with a *minko* ("chief") and a council who deliberated over important issues.[55] Keeping traditional ways alive has been an active endeavor thanks to Mississippi kin and the work of Rev. Eugene Wilson, who encouraged youth to learn traditional dances.[56] Traditional dances, language seminars, heritage classes, feasts of traditional foods, and stickball tournaments can all be experienced at the annual Choctaw Labor Day festival. The Labor Day festival also includes a language hymn singing, "This is our language, do not be ashamed of it."[57] Central to the Choctaw way of life is servant leadership, a way that has guided the Choctaw society for centuries.[58] This concept has influenced and guided tribal governments through times of difficulty and times of prosperity.

"The Utes word for their enemies was 'Komanticia' (or 'Kimaci') 'ones who fight me all the time' or 'enemy.'"[59] Comanche language is closely related to that of the Wyoming Shoshone tribe and has ties to the Uto-Aztecan language.[60] The Comanche people historically lived in most of present-day northwestern Texas and adjacent areas in eastern New Mexico, southeastern Colorado, southwestern Kansas, western Oklahoma, and northern Chihuahua before being relocated to the southwestern Lawton area of Oklahoma.[61] The Co-

54. "Choctaw People."
55. Clark, *Indian Tribes of Oklahoma*, 110.
56. Clark, *Indian Tribes of Oklahoma*, 110.
57. "Adeline Hudson."
58. "Servant Leadership."
59. Clark, *Indian Tribes of Oklahoma*, 121.
60. Clark, *Indian Tribes of Oklahoma*, 121.
61. Clark, *Indian Tribes of Oklahoma*, 123–24

manche people have a long and historic heritage as horsemen and warriors that begins early on in adolescence. Comanche boys are said to have learned to ride horses almost as soon as they learned to walk and were expected by the age of five to manage a pony and by six years of age to be fully skilled at riding horseback.[62] Since fathers were busy hunting and fighting, the boys' grandfathers would usually teach these skills as well as tribal history, traditions, legends, and religion.[63] "The Plains soldier tradition of the Comanches surfaced even during the early reservation period. Some worked as scouts at Fort Sill, and others later saw service in America's military wars overseas."[64] These times were always celebrated with men's society dances to the extent that the 1952 celebration of Korean War veterans became an annual homecoming and powwow.[65] Most notably, the Comanche are known for their deep connections with the buffalo and for their common title of the Lords of the Plains. Often called the *numu kutsu* (the Comanche Buffalo), the buffalo was more than a simple food source, but all the buffalos' parts were used in everyday life in some fashion.[66] In this way, the Comanche honored the sacrifice of the buffalo and was able to maximize the benefit for the effort in killing and cleaning the animal. This same practice was seen with other food sources of elk, deer, and antelope, while fish and waterfowl were seen as distasteful and were not eaten as other tribes did.[67] Comanche people pride themselves on their heritage and ceremonies that include traditional dances, feasts of traditional foods, unique regalia, and partnered dances with other tribes.

The Muscogee, also spelled Mvskoke, (Creek) Tribe of the current day eastern Oklahoma Okmulgee area originated from southern Tenessee, much of Alabama, western Georgia, and parts of northern Florida of the US. Some believe the term "Muscogee"

62. "Comanche Children."
63. "Comanche Children."
64. Clark, *Indian Tribes of Oklahoma*, 127.
65. Clark, *Indian Tribes of Oklahoma*, 127.
66. "Buffalo."
67. "Food Sources."

derives its name from the Shawnee word for "swamp."[68] Because of the linguistic relations to Western Muskhogean, the Muscogee tribe has connections with the Choctaw and Chickasaw Tribes. The Muscogee people were mound builders and have a history of migrating over large areas over time.[69] Traditional practices include powwows held in school gyms, festivals centered around dancing, singing, and feasting on traditional foods. Rituals often involve sacred fire at the center of towns or square grounds for annual ceremonies that often focus on giving thanks for the land, earth, and bounty and act as purification and renewal ceremonies.[70] Often these All-Night Dances attract many onlookers; one person recorded that the dancers were "violently stamping their feet" on the ground, giving light to the name Stomp Dance.[71] The annual Green Corn ceremony is a time of gathering to teach the language, preserve and teach the culture and traditions, as well as enjoy the bountiful harvest.

The Ponca name is unclear in its meaning but is believed to be a sub-name of a clan among the Kansas, Osages, and Quapaws.[72] Others find that the name Ponca is a combination of Siouan dialects and has more of a symbolic understanding of "sacred head."[73] The tribe is now based in north-central Oklahoma around Ponca City after removal from the Ohio, Mississippi, and Missouri regions of the US. "Poncas are related to other Dhegiha Siouan speakers like the Omahas, Osages, Kansas, and Quapaws."[74] Poncas reside in permanent earth-lodge villages with bands located along Ponca Creek and Verdel.[75] Historically the Ponca people have been extremely spiritual people with a vast range of rituals. To the Ponca people, *xube* (supernatural power) was everywhere

---

68. Clark, *Indian Tribes of Oklahoma*, 209.

69. Clark, *Indian Tribes of Oklahoma*, 212.

70. Clark, *Indian Tribes of Oklahoma*, 219.

71. Clark, *Indian Tribes of Oklahoma*, 19

72. Clark, *Indian Tribes of Oklahoma*, 279.

73. "Historic Tribes: Ponca."

74. Clark, *Indian Tribes of Oklahoma*, 280.

75. Clark, *Indian Tribes of Oklahoma*, 282.

and could be harnessed and shared by those who underwent a vision quest, particular rituals, or through medicine bundles.[76] The major tradition for the Ponca is the Sun Dance that preceded buffalo hunts as well as bundle rituals and renewal rituals that were primary to the summer months.[77] Interestingly, Poncas had priests that aided in these cleaning ceremonies and medicine lodges, similar to the Ojibwe Midewiwin. Lastly, the Ponca also held Pipe Dance (*Wa-wa*) as their Calumet Dance, which some believe to be introduced by the Pawnee people.[78] Ponca are a patrilineal tribe with clans and subclans all led by the head of the leading clan, who was in charge of caring for the tribal Pipe.[79] In the twentieth century, the Cheyenne and/or Tonkawa people introduced the Ponca to the Peyote religion where many have adapted a Half Moon version of the religion celebrated in a tipi around a sacred fire. Participants sing and pray in a circle following the guidance of a Roadman or Roadwoman. Specific songs are accompanied by a water drum with four parts to the ritual just as there are in the sweat lodge ritual. These four stages are represented by the red-hot coals, which are raked out and formed into designs.[80] Around the same time, the Ghost Dance was brought to the Ponca people as well as the Pawnee hand game.[81] "The Heduska (or Heouska) was an important Ponca warrior society dance. It was a war dance in which the male dancer wore a headdress and a Crow belt (bustle) that denoted membership and rank in the society. The women's version was called the Nuda. After the Poncas were confined to the reservation around 1880 the dance took on a religious aura, likely derived from the Dream or Drum dance of the era, which swept through the reservations."[82] Ponca people are still deeply tied to these traditions and practices as members are active in powwows,

76. Clark, *Indian Tribes of Oklahoma*, 282.
77. Clark, *Indian Tribes of Oklahoma*, 282.
78. Clark, *Indian Tribes of Oklahoma*, 280.
79. Clark, *Indian Tribes of Oklahoma*, 282.
80. Clark, *Indian Tribes of Oklahoma*, 285.
81. Clark, *Indian Tribes of Oklahoma*, 286.
82. Clark, *Indian Tribes of Oklahoma*, 286.

men play each other in games of shinny (which is a lacrosse-like contest played on a grassy field), and the people still enjoy Peyote ceremonies, dances, hand games, and more.[83]

One of the most recognizable and depicted tribes is the Seminole people known for their deep connections with Florida State University and their opening football game traditions. The name derives from the Muscogee (Creek) word *simanoli* or *siminoli* meaning "runaway" or "wild."[84] It is thought to be a reference to those who left or emigrated to settle elsewhere. Currently, the Seminole Tribe resides in central Oklahoma in Seminole County. The Seminole Tribe is originally derived from the Florida area of the US, which was also home to over sixty other tribes, giving Florida a rich and interestingly complex heritage.[85] Within the tribe, there are two prominent languages spoken. The Mikasuke of those in the Big Cypress area and the Muscogee of those in the Hollywood and Lake Okeechobee reservations.[86] The Seminole people are proud of their cultures and traditions, most notably their clothing, which is often made of colorful and recognizable multicolored designs on women's skirts and men's jackets called patchwork.[87] The designs represent the various symbols and images from Seminole heritage. The Seminole people have a long history with Christian missionaries who slowly but surely shaped the Seminole spiritual landscape. These Seminole churches were able to find a way to incorporate traditional practices and beliefs into their Christian practices with the use of language in sermons and hymns, the incorporation of a Seminole worldview, and even the building of churches facing the east, which aligned with traditional ceremonies.[88]

The tribes of Oklahoma are as different and yet similar at the same time as variations of fruits. With the sharing of traditions, the retaining of sacred identities, and what the changes of

83. Clark, *Indian Tribes of Oklahoma*, 287.

84. Clark, *Indian Tribes of Oklahoma*, 323.

85. Clark, *Indian Tribes of Oklahoma*, 323.

86. Clark, *Indian Tribes of Oklahoma*, 323.

87. Clark, *Indian Tribes of Oklahoma*, 323.

88. Clark, *Indian Tribes of Oklahoma*, 323.

the past several centuries have brought, Native American culture is an intertwined web of the utmost complexity. Where so many tribes share so much in common, at the same time the traditions and sacred practices couldn't be more different at times. The richness of the patchwork quilt that makes up the Oklahoma Indian community is a cultural wonder that begs to be appreciated and respected. From the Apache Fire Dance that is like no other to the Arapaho Ghost, Cherokee All-Night Dances, and Choctaw traditional dances, the culture is considerably diverse yet unified. From the Chickasaw sacred and traditional dishes to the horse culture of the Comanche and the medicine lodges of the depth of culture every tribe has to offer is a unique thread in the rich tapestry that is Native American culture in America.

SPIDERS AND RATTLESNAKES

I will never forget the day that my mother, after hearing about my rat race of a day as a kindergartner playing on the playground and learning the essentials to primary education, wanted to have a long talk with me. Having just heard of the playground shenanigans and daily activities of "playing cowboys and Indians," she told me that our family was indeed Indian and that I should be proud of who I am as a Native American. Naturally, the concept was lost due to my adolescence, but from that day forward I found myself playing different games on the playground and beginning a journey of self-discovery that would last the rest of my lifetime. That day my Chickasaw mother began to teach me the rich and sacred ways of our tribe and what it meant to be an Indian, a Chickasaw. These teachings I hold nearer and dearer to my heart than most things in life and I am so proud and thankful for how she has taught them to me so that I may live them out and share them with my children one day. The sad truth is, as rich and diverse as Native American cultures, traditions, and sacred ways of life are, they have been robbed and superficialized in unimaginable ways. The robbed traditions and gas station superficialism that has taken place over the last several decades is an indescribable and blatant injustice towards Native American peoples' customs, traditions, spirituality, and ways of life. From the stark inaccuracies and stereotypical influences of Hollywood to the growing culture of injustice that has allowed the perpetuation of the discriminatory and derogatory use of Native peoples' way of life, a social perspective of "other" towards Native American people has been created. The other truth is that Native people knew that their white counterparts would not only be coming for their land but would end up taking much more in their greed-filled campaign to own everything. "Our interpretation is he's a spider. The White Man's a spider and it's taken over everything. And his web is going to cover our lands. He's not going to stop."[89] Others have stated, "We perceive in them the cunning of the Rattlesnake who caresses the Squirrel he intends to devour."[90] From stealing lands to stealing sacred heritages and practices in unethical and disrespectful forms of self-pleasure, society has all but trivialized Native American culture to a mere gimmick in the eyes of so many.

Some of the stark stereotypes concerning Native American people stem so much from Hollywood. Julia Boyd argues that "one can use art, music, literature, television, and film to trace patterns in society."[91] Mrs. Boyd's work focuses on the stereotyping of Native Americans in film which permeates society in a rippling effect. For ages, Native Americans have been portrayed as violent, savage, uncivilized, and ruthless killers of few words with magical powers. While the media often depicts Indigenous men as warriors and magical healers, females are habitually portrayed as beautiful objects of desire. Often the portrayal of Native Americans is of a stoic, unsmiling, emotionless one-dimensional figure lacking the ability to resonate emotionally on any level. Mrs. Boyd identifies this as the noble savage persona credited to Jacquelyn Kilpatrick's work *Celluloid Indians*.[92] This unrealistic perception negates the true humor and deep range of emotions in which Native American

89. "Blood of the Ground."
90. "Yammat sishto-at chimmi fannat apachitok."
91. Boyd, "Examination of Native Americans," 105.
92. Boyd, "Examination of Native Americans," 106.

people feel just as any other human groups do. In many ways, this stoic portrayal furthers the negation of humanity in Native American peoples that has existed since European contact. "Contemporary popular representation of Indians such as *Pocahontas* (1995) or *The Last of The Mohicans* (1992) put the spotlight on Indians, but there is still very little valuable or authentic information about the history or culture of contemporary Native Americans."[93] She goes on to highlight how films like *Nanook of the North*, with its false narrative as a documentary, and *Little Big Man*, with its revisionist take on blanketing Native Americans, all work to create a dichotomy in the society of Native American peoples.[94] One of the earliest examples is the 1953 film *Peter Pan*, which many believe gave the impression that Native peoples were unable to communicate outside of outlandish nonverbal means. The film negates the advancement of Native American civilizations and clear means of communicating, evidently seen in the rich diplomacy in the early trade organizations. Another example is the 2013 remake of *The Lone Ranger*, featuring Indigenous sidekick Tonto played by Johnny Depp. The film used red paint on faces to darken the skin color, giving non-Native actor Johnny Depp a more "Native" feel. This is a prime example of the whitewashing that takes place in films with Indigenous peoples all the time. Whitewashing is the use of white actors and actresses for roles that were not designed for them to play. When whitewashing takes place, it furthers the colonial and European mentality of the incapability of Native American people in society. Martin Berny argues that Hollywood loves to exploit the miscegenation of the time and the cowboy versus Indians opposition of the early nineteenth and twentieth centuries.[95] The Hollywood portrayal of Native Americans created a brushfire that swept the world as Native Americans became icons of stereotypical mantras.

What Hollywood started and created has become a sweeping motion that has resulted in the identification of Native American

93. Boyd, "Examination of Native Americans," 107.

94. Boyd, "Examination of Native Americans," 107.

95. Berny, "Hollywood Indian Stereotype," 14.

culture and way of life as a caricatured manifestation that crudely mimics and mocks traditional practices and ways of life. "Commercial exploitation of Native American spiritual traditions has permeated the New Age movement since its emergence in the 1980s. Euro-Americans professing to be medicine people have profited from publications and workshops. Mass quantities of products promoted as 'Native American sacred objects' have been successfully sold by white entrepreneurs to a largely non-Indian market."[96] Lisa Aldred in her article "Plastic Shamans and Astroturf Sun Dances" draws attention to the misuse of Native American culture and traditions in the forms of plastic medicine people, Native American tarot cards, cheap means of mimicked sweat lodges, neo-tribal spiritualism, shopping mall lifestyle trends, noble savage escapism, Indian fetishizations, and overall commercialization.[97] These inauthentic and inaccurate renderings of what it means to be Native American are a cautionary tale to the true spirituality that can be learned from Native peoples. Traditional healing ceremonies have been mimicked with cheap means of healing and wholeness that undermined the spiritual and serious aspects of Native American botanical beliefs and practices. Historic images of Native peoples have been distorted and disfigured to match the more savage mentality of Indian men or the lustful oversexualized mentality of Indian women. Iconic and sacred items like dreamcatchers could be found in cheap recreations with unrealistic designs in gas stations far and wide with stickers on them stating "made in China." Traditional dresses and regalia became a satirized and sexualized form of entertainment for Halloween and dress-up occasions. Traditional songs and drumming nuances have been used by non-Native teachers in vulgar efforts to teach high school algebra.[98] Native spirituality with nature has been used in sardonic and inaccurate depictions and crude reenactments.

"After all this time stereotypes and lies about us persist in contemporary society, blurring the true picture of our people. The

96. Aldred, *Plastic Shamans and Astroturf Sun Dances,* 329.

97. Aldred, "Plastic Shamans," 347.

98. Downey, "After Riverside Teacher's Mock."

lies make us invisible. They make us doubt our self-worth. What can a person do? We answer with our unique Indian sense of humor. We poke fun at the stereotypes and show how absurd they are."[99] One of the best depictions of the misrepresentation of Native American way of life can be seen at the First Americans Museum in Oklahoma City. The large museum depicts elements of Native American culture and meaning, as deep as the number of stones that make up the grand entryway to the mound that aligns with the solstice calendars and the grand archway that depicts a giant dreamcatcher illuminating the Oklahoma City skyline. In the historical exhibit, the Wall of Misrepresentations is a draw for Native and non-Native alike. The wall depicts historic misrepresentations of Native American culture and traditions over the centuries. Saltshakers with overly large-nosed dark skin replications of Indian men adorned in inaccurate and embellished regalia and pictures of professional wrestlers flying over a wrestling ring with a sign that reads, "Merciless Indian Savages" adorn this eye-catching and breathtaking wall exhibit. A sign of notable disrespectful names and phrases for Native peoples reads, "Cigar store Indian. Drunk Indian. Noble, stoic brave. 'Going off the reservation.' Uncivilized heathens. Primitive. Redskin. 'Hey Chief!' Geronimo! 'On the warpath.' The natives are restless."[100] Phrases that have been used with hate and vengeance at times to hurt and ridicule Native American people and our sacred ways of life. Playing Indian is another staple of this display with an explanation that reads, "Playing Indian began with the Boston Tea Party when colonists dressed up as Indians and dumped tea into the harbor. Closer to home, 'Playing Indian' was often part of the program celebrating the anniversary of Oklahoma's statehood. Dressing up as an Indian stereotype—often the 'Noble savage' or provocative 'Indian Maiden'—continues into the 21st century. These impersonations allow non-Natives to live out racist fantasies."[101]

99. "Wall of Misrepresentations."
100. "Wall of Misrepresentations."
101. "Wall of Misrepresentations."

WALL OF STEREOTYPES[102]

The harm that these perpetuations do to the Native American community is far deeper and more severe than most can imagine. "Playing Indian," derogatory gestures, inaccurate and cartoonish personifications, and caricatured stereotypes only serve to propagate the racist, discriminatory, oppressive, and marginalizing mentalities of Native Americans begun by European colonists and sustained into our current times and context. Michael Yellow Bird emphasizes the struggle with toys in American society that symbolize the genocide of Native American people with little to no regard for the harm they have had towards Native American people.[103]

NO LONGER BUGS

While attending an immersion with the Oklahoma Indian Missionary Conference in the summer of 2021, as part of my research, I encountered a passionate and motivated Ponca woman who

102. "Wall of Misrepresentations."
103. Yellow Bird, "Cowboys and Indians," 33.

spoke about the Missing and Murdered Indigenous Peoples movement, which works against the harm being done to Native people. While impressing upon a largely non-Native group of people the realities of what is happening in communities concerning missing Indigenous persons, the woman spoke briefly about what Natives go through daily in the larger social context. She passionately asked the group if we could imagine walking into a restaurant, shopping place, or local grocery store and being looked at like we were bugs that no one wanted there. The words were sobering for the many participants that have no idea what the daily realities of being Native American are like. This woman's wise and pain-filled words are a testament to the mentality that must be broken for progress to begin. It is this mentality that must be broken for the work of appreciating and living more deeply with God through a Native American perspective to take place at all.

The harsh and derogatory place that society has found itself in and the racist and discriminatory biases towards Native Americans looms largely from a colonial and evangelistic mindset. Colonists came to convert Native Americans with the preconceived notions that Native American cultures, traditions, and ways of life were uncivilized, savage, and crude. The reality is this is far from the truth. Without European, Spanish, or any other contact or influences, Native peoples would be living traditional ways just as successfully and fruitfully as we have for the centuries before first contact. Many would argue that without this contact, much more would be retained than what was lost due to these outside influences. Where colonists moved to culture the Natives, evangelists had been trying to save the Natives. The question to ask is, from what? Native Americans lived spiritually rich lives before contact and articulated a clear and resolute understanding of God as the Creator. Many Native people believe the gift of Christianity was in a deepening of this faith through an understanding of Jesus Christ and the loving acts of God for all peoples. Where things went wrong is where earlier Christians missed the spirituality, faith, and Christianity right before their eyes, resulting in a work of conversion that was not only unnecessary to the extent that it took place but was also unethical. The ultimate result was a deep chasm between Native American tradition and Christianity, which created a lasting struggle between the two practices to this very day. Early evangelistic tactics seen in the Indian boarding schools, in missionary efforts, and inside church walls centered on changing the Native instead of working to build from what was already present. Some argue that a separation between Native and non-Native might be the best possible step forward. Inés Hernández-Ávila approaches Native American spirituality from her descent and culture. She is of Nimipu and Tejano cultural backgrounds that both strongly influence her understanding and appreciation of Native American culture and spiritual traditions. Mrs. Avila describes that there is a certain challenge for Native people when revealing their spiritual practices. There is a hesitation based on the bias, stereotyping, misunderstanding, and lack of appreciation that has taken place in the past. She writes,

> At what price does the revealing of Danza, or any ceremony, happen so that the world (and/or the academy) can "share" in the experience, given that the world tends to dismiss any ethical considerations in the fervor of "discovery." I agree with Sequoya when she suggests, "Perhaps one might consider such dismissive strategies as an institutional residue of the paradigm of the vanishing Indian[s]" who are objectified rather than recognized as subject and voice of their own stories.[104]

Mrs. Avila is not alone in the mindset of letting Indian people be so they can continue to live without the constant and persistent oppressive and pejorative acts toward our peoples and cultural identities. At what cost (many would argue total decimation) does it take for the stereotypical and discriminatory treatment of Native peoples to end? For Mrs. Avila, there is a constant struggle and back-and-forth shifting between Americanism and Native Americanism that is slowly working to dilute and diminish the presence of Native American spirituality. Avila claims that for Native

---

104. Hernández-Ávila, "Mediations of the Spirit," 332. Brackets in the original.

American spirituality to thrive in its authenticity, there must be an end to the lack of rights for Native people to practice their beliefs as much as any other religion. There must also be an end to the consumerism that plagues non-Native people's approach to Native American objects, spiritual practices, culture, and identity. The more that is shared the more that is misconstrued, abused, and stereotyped, which has created a strong sense of hesitation for Native American people to reveal what is sacred and what is received and portrayed as hokey and simply negating its sacred aspects. The evangelistic "Kill the Indian, and Save the Man"[105] mentality ultimately destroyed many ways of communing with God that the Christian church needed, needs, and will forever need.

One way to engage this work in a sacred way is to begin to see Native American people for who we are and the very real struggles that are faced every single day. One often misunderstood stereotype is Native Americans' battle with alcoholism. The work of Rosalie Torres Stone, Les B. Whitbeck, Xiajin Chen, Kurt Johnson, and Debbie M. Olson looks more closely into this phenomenon with an eye towards real causes and real solutions. They write, "Numerous contextual factors contribute to the high rates of alcohol misuse and dependency among Native Indian adults. Recent studies indicate that heavy drinking is associated with being male, being young, having less than a high school diploma, and being unemployed."[106] Ultimately they argue that alcoholism is a real and prevalent issue that cannot be simplified to genetics but that it is largely contextual and that a greater method of healing should look to incorporate Native American worldviews and spiritual practices, which will produce greater cessation.[107] Where alcoholism is but one issue concerning Native American communities and is shown to be the result of contextual situations, it proves that there are deep and serious concerns happening within Native American communities that the outside world refuses and cares not to see. Likewise, suicide is a prevalent situation that

105. Patterson, "Pastor Reflects on Abuses," para. 7.
106. Torres et al., "Traditional Practices, Traditional Spirituality," 237.
107. Torres et al., "Traditional Practices, Traditional Spirituality," 243.

needs healing and wholeness within Native American communities. Eva Marie Garroute, Jack Goldberg, Janette Beals, Richard Herrell, Spero M. Manson, and the AI-SUPERPFP Team of Boston Colleges Sociology department recognize that American Indians show suicide-related behaviors at rates far greater than the general population.[108] The group highlight that "rates of attempted suicide is extremely high among American Indians, ranging from 15% to 31% in some tribes or tribal subpopulations."[109] The group resolves that spiritual commitment reveals higher emotional well-being resulting in lowered suicide attempts.[110] They further conclude that the involvement of spiritual practice from a Native American perspective could be crucial in the healing and wholeness programs offered to those struggling with suicidal tendencies or motivations.[111] Another area is the reality that Native American people go missing every single day without the same reporting, care, and attention that other groups see when missing. This occurrence grew to the point that Native people began to take matters into their own hands to help find these persons as they go missing. This tension came to a head recently as Gabby Petito went missing on September 11, 2021, sparking national media attention and an all-out reaction from Native American communities. For years Indigenous people have gone missing in the same area with little to no consideration, but a Caucasian girl of the same age goes missing and it sparks national news only to serve as a painful reminder that the importance of Native Americans in society is not of equal value to so many people. The humbling and sad truth is that Native women are missing and murdered in stark numbers every single day with little to no recognition from larger organizations or media. Native American men, children, and elders go missing for a myriad of reasons daily with little to no attention or care.

Native Americans are not bugs. We are people of sacred value and holy worth and have a way of viewing the world and living

108. Garoutte et al., "Spirituality and Attempted Suicide," 1571.

109. Garoutte et al., "Spirituality and Attempted Suicide," 1571.

110. Garoutte et al., "Spirituality and Attempted Suicide," 1576.

111. Garoutte et al., "Spirituality and Attempted Suicide," 1577.

life in connection with God that many could benefit from. The starting place is here, to see Native people as human beings that Standing Bear fought so hard for years and years ago. "This hand is not the color of yours, but if I pierce it, I shall feel pain. If you pierce your hand, you also feel pain. The blood that will flow from mine will be of the same color as yours. I am a man. The same God made us both."[112] We want to be seen and treated with the same respect and dignity as everyone else. We want to matter, and we want to have the same opportunities and privileges as anyone else. This is the starting point, to see Native American people as human beings who deserve the same decency and respect that anyone else deserves. When this takes place and Native people can be seen as human and worthy, then the sacred work can begin to learn from our traditional ways. When Native people can be seen as human, then the spiritual way of living that is inherent to who we are can be shared with all those that bask in the sun of the Creator. When Native people can be seen as human, a mindset can emerge that opens limitless opportunities in communing with God.

112. "Standing Bear Monument."

III

What Is Spirituality?

THE MAN THAT CAME into my office that day beckoned me to provide spiritual practice after spiritual practice hoping for a magic cure-all or fix-all. The breakdown occurred not in the desperation and longing of the parishioner who sought aid to their situation, it was in the lack of clarity that constitutes spirituality in the first place. Often spirituality is seen as either a quick and easy means of curing or aiding a longing within or is seen as so abstract that they feel spirituality is only for the select, or even elect, few. Both notions contradict both Christian and Native American concepts of spirituality, and the importance of living spiritually is for daily life. Before a conversation can develop about the intersectionality between Native American and Christian spirituality, a clear understanding must be formed of what constitutes spirituality. There are many different and often competing notions of what exactly spirituality is and the different views on how it is manifested. Within the Christian realm, many different views are denominationally separated and theologically separated. Outside of the Christian realm, there is an even broader array of views and concepts involved. To say the topic is complex is an understatement and begs clarification for this project. Where there are notable differences within and between the Native American and Christian communities concerning spirituality, there are notable intersectionality points that implore attention.

From a Christian perspective, spirituality is often fraught with misconceptions and false notions. Some Christians find that they don't connect well with typical or traditional means of spiritual practices and thus resolve that they are not spiritual. This misconception deals more with the lack of connecting with a resonating praxis instead of the deeper concept of spirituality itself. As many will argue, spirituality is not a gift bestowed on certain Christians like preaching can be, but has more to do with daily living in deep connection with God that leads to intentional practices that help garner this relationship. Another misconception is that spirituality will magically fix whatever internal ailments are happening. This misconception undermines the understanding of spirituality as daily communion with God and negates the work and effort that goes into spiritual living—surely a product of our century's "bang for the buck" mentality that seeks high gratification with little to no effort. Both misconceptions stand as immense hurdles before a life of spiritual living can take place and flourish.

CHRISTIAN SPIRITUALITY

From a Christian approach, spirituality has a long and complicated past. Even before the time of Jesus Christ, living spiritually with God was present. Adam and Eve in Gen 1–2 arguably lived in the most communal way possible as they resided in the garden of Eden and lived with God. Abraham spoke often with God and exemplified obedience in degrees admired to this day. King David, although not the most obedient, is said to have a heart after God's own heart. Noah communicated and worked with God in building the ark. Moses spoke often with God and lived close to God in his endeavor to lead the Israelite people out of Egypt and out from under the oppressive hand of Pharaoh. The prophets all beckoned Israel to seek a closer relationship with God through loving obedience to God and care for neighbors. "But those who hope in the Lord will renew their strength. They will soar on the wings like eagles; they will run and not grow weary, they will walk and not be faint" (Isa 40:31). Naturally, Jesus's ministry brings a profound understanding as he says, "Abide in me, and I in you. As the branch cannot bear fruit by itself, unless it abides in the vine, neither can you, unless you abide in me" (John 15:4 NKJV) and that "man shall not live by bread alone, but by every word that comes from the mouth of God" (Matt 4:4 ESV). He also says, "Have faith in God. Truly, I say to you, whoever says to this mountain, 'Be taken up and thrown into the sea,' and does not doubt in his heart, but believes that what he says will come to pass, it will be done for him. Therefore, I tell you, whatever you ask in prayer, believe that you have received it, and it will be yours" (Mark 11:22–24 ESV). In Luke's Gospel a clearer understanding of spirituality comes through Jesus's words on the kingdom as he proclaims, "The kingdom of God is not coming with signs to be observed, nor will they say, 'Look, here it is!' or 'There!' for behold, the kingdom of God is in the midst of you" (Luke 17:20–21 ESV). Later James 4:8 says, "Come close to God, and God will come close to you. Wash your hands, you sinners; purify your hearts, for your loyalty, is divided between God and the world" (NLT). Jude follows this up with these challenging words: "But you, beloved, building yourselves up in your most holy faith and praying in the Holy Spirit, keep yourselves in the love of God, waiting for the mercy of our Lord Jesus Christ that leads to eternal life" (Jude 1:20–21 ESV). The Pauline Epistles deal largely with the concept of spirituality as a pillar for the Christian life. Paul implores the church in Galatia, "But if you bite and devour one another, watch out that you are not consumed by one another. But I say, walk by the Spirit, and you will not gratify the desires of the flesh. For the desires of the flesh are against the Spirit, and the desires of the Spirit are against the flesh, for these are opposed to each other, to keep you from doing the things you want to do" (Gal 5:15–17 ESV). Most popularly and accurately, Paul highlights the marks of spiritual living as "by contrast, the fruit of the Spirit is love, joy, peace, patience, kindness, generosity, faithfulness, gentleness, and self-control. There is no law against such things" (Gal 5:22–23 NLT). He also instructs the church of Rome to "let love be genuine. Abhor what is evil; hold fast to what is good. Love one another with brotherly affection. Outdo one another in showing honor. Do not be slothful in zeal, be fervent in spirit, serve the Lord. Rejoice in hope, be patient in tribulation, be constant in prayer. Contribute to the needs of the saints and seek to show hospitality" (Rom 12:9–21 ESV). Although this is only a brief glimpse of the considerably large understanding a biblical approach provides to spirituality, it can easily be concluded that spiritual living includes a deep and passionate life lived constantly connected with God. A life when God begins to undergird every action, thought, word, and essence of who we are is a life of deep spiritual living. The result, as noted in many of the previous Scriptures, is a life lived in love of God and neighbor that emanates obedience and faith, daily finding peace, hope, and joy in this relationship with the divine. Where the oldest understanding of spiritual living is drawn from holy Scripture, the church's tradition and various theologians over the centuries have aided in this interpretation.

For centuries people believed that the Latin words in the Catholic mass of *hoc est enim corpus meum,* or loosely translated as "hocus pocus," were the magical words said over the elements that magically transformed them into the actual body and blood of Christ. Although this belief is in no way accurate to Roman Catholic (or any other mainline) sacramental understanding, it serves as a wonderful example of the magical and mystical premonitions that often surround spirituality in the Christian tradition. From a Christian perspective there is a deep and thorough tradition of what constitutes spirituality that finds its essence from a biblical perspective.

> "For all who are led by the Spirit of God are children of God. . . .When we cry, 'Abba! Father!' it is that very Spirit bearing witness with our spirit that we are children of God" (Rom. 8: 14–16). Although the apostle Paul never uses the word "spirituality," this earnest confession of faith suggests that any Christian understanding of that term must necessarily refer to the intimate loving relationship

between God's Holy Spirit and the spirit (animating life force) of believers—a relationship that can be characterized both as kinship and as communion.[1]

While this definition in its broadness does highlight central aspects of Christian spirituality, the reality is that this topic is both deep and wide in its range of understandings. The term "spirituality" itself is defined within the common English dialect in terms of living a certain lifestyle.[2] Adele Ahlberg Calhoun in her book *Spiritual Disciplines Handbook: Practice That Transforms Us* writes, "A spiritual practice isn't magic. It won't change you by itself, but it puts you in a place to partner with the Holy Spirit to become an ever-fresh *eikon* of Jesus."[3] Calhoun is describing a fundamental misguidance many people suffer from when it comes to the spiritual but not religious movement of today's culture.

Seeking God in All Things: Theology and Spiritual Direction by William Reiser is a theologically deep and vast read that encounters the art of spiritual direction and the theological concepts that undergird this practice. At the forefront is Mr. Reiser's concept of "Where do holy things come from?" and his understanding that this is best revealed through the Christian church. Here Mr. Reiser claims that it is the family structure, liturgical basis, and practice of preaching that divulge the sincerest desire for God. Mr. Reiser casually integrates a biblical narrative, avowing, "Where such an atmosphere is lacking, the search for God is going to resemble a philosopher's search for truth and enlightenment—Magi without a star."[4] He adds that "the desire for God, I would conclude, is essentially an ecclesial desire—a desire rendered possible by the existence of a community of faith."[5] Mr. Reiser is adamant that it is easy to slip into the mindset of "spiritual direction is a pious and solitary event" when, in its most authentic nature, it is social. Spiritual direction comes from a longing to not only love and

1. Holder, *Blackwell Companion to Christian Spirituality*, 1.
2. Holder, *Blackwell Companion to Christian Spirituality*, 2.
3. Calhoun, *Spiritual Disciplines Handbook*, 11.
4. Reiser, *Seeking God in All Things*, 61.
5. Reiser, *Seeking God in All Things*, 62.

experience God but to also engage in a community of believers. It gives new depth to the Matt 22:36–40 Scripture of the greatest commandment; Jesus was speaking more to our deepest and truest desires as spiritual people and not just our obligation in carrying out the *Missio Dei*. Our deepest desire for God and community reflects our eschatological hope in Jesus Christ. Reiser highlights that Ignatian expression to "find God in all things."[6] Mr. Reiser's work is crucial to the work of Native American spirituality in that it sets the precedent of the innate desire to know God and be in relationship with both God and community. Biblically this aligns with Paul's visit to the Areopagus where he finds an altar to the "unknown god" (Acts 17:22–31). Paul stands up and claims that this is only a reflection of their longing to know the true God of all creation, the God of Abraham and Isaac. Paul proclaimed, "Men of Athens, I perceive that in every way you are very religious. For as I passed along and observed the object of your worship, I also found an altar with the inscription: 'To the unknown god.' What therefore you worship as unknown, this I proclaim to you" (Acts 17:22–23 NKJV). Mr. Reiser's text also reflects the theological concept of human anthropology and the innate need to be in a community. As the Triune God, a social God created humankind in God's image (Gen 1:26–28), so are we created to reflect this social aspect of God who is in constant relationship with all of creation. These two concepts together reveal the need for a spiritual life that allows the relationship with God to flourish in the life of believers. This also sets the precedent to be in community or "tribe." This tribal mentality is an important concept to adopting a "Native" outlook to spiritual living. Knowing that this desire to be in "tribe" comes from a congenital place of our created identity is essential. Mr. Reiser's work emphasizes what Bonhoeffer and Neafsey are claiming that to answer the call of God (Neafsey) and live fully into that calling (Bonhoeffer), a strong spiritual life must be present. It also parallels Richardson's work on ancestry as Reiser claims the need for community. These two aspects of "tribe" speak with each other as a foundational part to healthy, holy, and wholly living.

6. Reiser, *Seeking God in All Things*, 65.

James N. Nelson describes spirituality in common understandings as an endeavor for the transcendent.[7] For Mr. Nelson, spirituality is a difficult term to narrow down, but definitions that focus on singular aspects of spirituality undermine the multifaceted nature of the topic and the various layers that any one decent definition should offer. Overall Mr. Nelson argues that where spirituality can be void of religion in most definitions and understandings, this is rather difficult.[8] Where spirituality has found a secular nuance in today's current spiritual climate, it generally tends to deal more with a connection with the divine in most cases as a means of fulfillment and purpose.[9] Many cultures and traditions find this term as a descriptor of what naturally takes place in the everyday life for the people of that community. For example, for many in the Chickasaw tradition, living a life in a deep relationship with Ababinili (Creator) is not a life deemed or termed spiritual, it is simply the way Chickasaw people live their lives. Thus, for centuries the term spirituality has been a term referencing the normal practices of deep connection and relationship with God. Sandra M. Schneiders argues that "first, spirituality is not simply spontaneous experience, however elevating or illuminating, but a conscious and deliberate way of living. It is an ongoing project, not merely a collection of experiences or episodes. Thus, lived spirituality is often referred to as one's 'spiritual life.'"[10] Domenec Mele and Joan Fontradona argue the same point in their article "Christian Ethics and Spirituality in Leading Business Organizations: Editorial Introduction":

> Spirituality is that which animates a person's life of faith and moves a person's faith to greater depths and perfection. It is a way of life which entails beliefs and values related with an ultimate concern. For Christians, the ultimate concern is God revealed in Jesus Christ, and Christian spirituality requires the fellowship of Christ and living in Christ through the gift of the Holy Spirit. Spirituality

7. Nelson, *Psychology, Religion, and Spirituality*, 8.

8. Nelson, *Psychology, Religion, and Spirituality*, 10.

9. Nelson, *Psychology, Religion, and Spirituality*, 12.

10. Quoted in Holder, *Blackwell Companion to Christian Spirituality*, 16.

involves the whole person (body, mind, soul, relationships), the entire fabric of our lives; it is a lived experience
and involves experiencing and knowing God (not just
knowing about God).[11]

This concept of spirituality as a permeation of one's entire self is
fundamental to both the Christian and Native American views of
spirituality and will be crucial when developing a mindset needed
to approach spiritual living in the intersection between these two
communities.

Historically and theologically the church mystics, such
as Dionysius, Thomas Aquinas, and John of the Cross, have approached spirituality from a perspective that largely deals with the
supernatural aspects. "John of the Cross says: 'The sweet and living
knowledge that she [the soul] says he [God] taught her is mystical
theology, the secret knowledge of God that spiritual persons call
contemplation' (The Spiritual Canticle 27: 5)."[12] Naturally, as Christian denominations began to form due to conflicts and differences
theologically, so did a variety of opinions of what characterized
Christian spirituality. Sacramental, ecclesiological, soteriological,
pneumatological, christological, and anthropological differences
and separation paved the way for a broad understanding of spirituality to take root. One notable advancement was the increased
missional efforts of later Christianity that produced a prophetic
spirituality centered on bringing about justice. As theological posi-
tions such as liberation, feminism, and womanism have emerged,
there has been a deep calling for social justice to be at the forefront
of spirituality. Walt Whitman wrote in 1871,

> Judging from the main portions of the history of the
> world so far, justice is always in jeopardy, peace walks
> amid hourly pitfalls and of slavery, misery, meanness,
> the craft of tyrants and the credulity of the populace, in
> some of their protean forms, no voice can at any time say,
> "They are not pervasive." The cloud breaks a little and the

11. Mele, and Fontradona, "Christian Ethics and Spirituality," 673.

12. Holder, *Blackwell Companion to Christian Spirituality*, 22. Brackets in
the original.

> sun shines out but soon and certain the lowering darkness falls again as if to last forever. Yet is there an immortal courage and prophesy in every sane soul that must, under any circumstances capitulate. Viva the attack! The perennial assault. Viva the unpopular cause, the spirit that audaciously aims, the never abandoned effort pursued the same amid opposing proofs and precedents.[13]

Mr. Whitman's words echo this justice-fronted spirituality and exemplify one of many variations to what embodies spirituality.

Another take is a Wesleyan perspective of Methodist and similar denominations that lean on the teachings of John Wesley. Elaine Heath in her book *Five Means of Grace: Experiencing God's Love the Wesleyan Way* shares a story of a woman who loved to iron and found a connection with God through the act of ironing.[14] This form of spirituality connects deeply with an understanding that all things can be spiritual when involving God. The premise is that God can and will use any and every source possible as avenues of grace in our lives so that we may live more deeply in communion with God. The Roman Catholic church has different historic orders that have greatly influenced how spirituality is lived out. Several of these include the Franciscans, founded by St. Francis of Assisi, who are known for living the gospel, following Jesus Christ, living a life of poverty, and having a strong sense of fraternity;[15] the Carthusians, founded by St. Bruno of Cologne, whose spirituality is evident in acts of contemplation, solitude, simplicity, and sobriety;[16] and the Jesuits, founded by St. Ignatius of Loyola, who understand spiritual living as finding God in everything, deeply loving Jesus Christ, emphasizing the importance of service, spiritual discernment, and prominence of education.[17] The current pope, Pope Francis, believes that spirituality and leadership go hand in hand.[18] Spirituality in the

---

13. Quoted in West, *Prophetic Thought in Postmodern Times*, 204.

14. Heath, *Five Means of Grace*, vii–viii.

15. Currier, *History of Religious Orders*, 18.

16. Currier, *History of Religious Orders*, 18.

17. Currier, *History of Religious Orders*, 22.

18. Lowney, *Pope Francis*, 11.

pope's life is not a set of practices that he pulls out when needed or wanted, but it is an undergirding of everything he does so that he is more faithful in all aspects of his life. Chris Lowney writes, "I have never met the Pope, but I suspect that he doesn't even have a 'leadership philosophy'—instead, he focuses on one priority only: he is a follower of Jesus, and his Jesuit formation helps him follow Jesus more closely, end of the story."[19] The Benedictine Order, founded by St. Benedict of Nursia, stresses a spiritual life of prayer and daily manual work, rigorous practice of reading Scripture and the Divine Office, a strong sense of community life and fraternal love, and overwhelming obedience as discernment of God's will.[20] Augustinians, founded by Pope Innocent IV considering the great St. Augustus, characterize spiritual living as deeply living the gospel and the liturgy, communion of life, the search for God and interiority, apostolic activities according to the needs of the church, and the study and the cultivation of knowledge.[21] Lastly, the Carmelites began as a community of hermits on Mount Carmel, Palestine, inspired by prophet Elijah. Their rule was approved by Pope Innocent IV, and they lived by a rule of contemplation and prayer (modeling the life and faith of Mary and the prophet Elijah), fraternity, and a deep sense of service.[22] For German theologian Dietrich Bonhoeffer, spiritual care is rooted in the theological principle of the love of God. To proclaim the Lord is to proclaim love. Proclamation is ministering to people in need, and this is divine. It is a gift from God to humanity. Thus, proclamation is to provide that God is our help and comforter, but also Christ in his victory is a victory over sickness, death, pain, and suffering, and that forgiveness was provided on the cross. This proclamation is the mission of spiritual care, which is the mission and ministry to proclaim the word, both of which Bonhoeffer sees as being linked.[23] The work of Dietrich Bonhoeffer goes to show the central focus that strong spirituality is

19. Lowney, *Pope Francis*, 11.

20. Currier, *History of Religious Orders*, 23.

21. Currier, *History of Religious Orders*, 22.

22. Currier, *History of Religious Orders*, 18.

23. Bonhoeffer, *Spiritual Care*, 48.

needed to undergird the life of every Christian. Whether proclaiming the gospel of Jesus Christ or hearing the gospel, there is a great need for spiritual care. Sin either hinders the ability to proclaim the gospel or hear the gospel and this sin can only be battled with spiritual care, in Bonhoeffer's opinion. Similarly, John Neafsey writes in *A Sacred Voice Is Calling: Personal Vocation and Social Conscience* that the precise point of love must be at the root of all that we do as Christian believers and this is not only a commandment of our Lord and Savior but is a calling that exists upon all who claim Jesus Christ as Lord and Savior. When love is the motivating factor in our lives, our most authentic and most sacred calling is answered, and our lives become a beautiful expression of the love and grace of God manifested in the life, death, and resurrection of Jesus Christ. Mr. Neafsey focuses on several significant points, underpinning the act of hearing, discerning, and responding to this sacred calling. It is through personal vocation and social consciousness, listening, understanding the heart, creating an authentic expression, uplifting passion and compassion, visioning, suffering, and understanding conscience that this sacred calling is lived out.

At the heart of hearing, discerning, and responding to this sacred calling is a love of learning and learning to love, hearing the cry of the needy and responding in love, and an authentic reaction that refuses imitation but resonates with the love of the saints. Mr. Neafsey points out the claim Thomas Groome makes in *Educating for Life: A Spiritual Vision for Every Teacher and Parent*, that orthodoxies be met with a profound sense of orthopraxis as "we 'consider the worthiest purpose of education as that learners might become fully alive human beings who help to create a society that serves the common good.'"[24] John Neafsey focuses on several significant points underpinning the act of hearing, discerning, and responding to this sacred calling. This is best illustrated in the closing prayer Mr. Neafsey uses, saying, "Oh God, I thank you for having created me as I am, I thank you for the sense of fulfillment I sometimes have: that fulfillment is, after all, nothing but being filled with You. I promise You to strive my whole life long for beauty and harmony

24. Neafsey, *Sacred Voice Is Calling*, 17.

and also humility and true love, whispers of which I hear inside me during my best moments."[25] "Christian spirituality in the modern period is often seen as characterized by a decline in the mystical tradition and the spiritual disciplines and devotional practices of Christendom."[26] This is a concept that will be explored more in-depth later on, but goes to show the ends result of a long and arduous past as the continuously shifting sands of the Christian church have produced a chasm in the connection between spirituality as a daily and habitual part of life, instead of the magic cure-all that so many abuse it into being today. At the heart of hearing, discerning, and responding to this sacred calling is a love of learning and learning to love, hearing the cry of the needy and responding in love, and an authentic reaction that refuses imitation but resonates with the love of the saints. This is our sacred calling; this is love living and breathing in the world today.

NATIVE AMERICAN SPIRITUALITY

The Christian understanding of spirituality, although broad and sometimes diverse, highlights the central aspect that spirituality involves a lifelong connection with God as the center and root of our entire lives. Dick Houtman and Stef Aupers argue this in saying, "This, then, is the main tenant of post-Christian spirituality: the belief that in the deepest layers of the self the 'divine spark'— to borrow a term from ancient Gnosticism—is still smoldering, waiting to be stirred up, and succeed the socialized self. Getting in touch with this 'true,' 'deeper,' or 'divine' self is not considered a 'quick fix,' but rather understood as a long-term process."[27]

Many might expect that a Native American perspective will undermine or contradict this understanding, but as research shows, the two communities share more commonalities than they ever do distinctions. Lee Irwin defines this by saying,

25. Neafsey, *Sacred Voice Is Calling*, 177.

26. Holder, *Blackwell Companion to Christian Spirituality*, 153.

27. Houtman and Aupers, "Spiritual Turn," 306–307.

Perhaps the word "spiritual" needs clarification. My own understanding of spirituality in this context is something more than simply practicing a particular religion. This word "religion" doesn't sit well either in such context, being as it is a post-enlightenment concept often rooted in a polarity between ideas of the "sacred and profane." Such a distinction is an artificial and non-helpful locus for understanding the primary foundations of Native spirituality. My own experience of the interactive spheres of Native communal life is that they have a relatedness through personal relationships that finds common expression in mutual, everyday concerns.[28]

John Neafsey writes, "When we move in the right direction, we feel right with God and with ourselves. Inwardly, we experience the sense of intuitive 'rightness,' that accompanies any step we take in the direction of emotional and spiritual health and growth. We feel healthy when we are moving in the right direction; the path feels right to us."[29] Neafsey's work is steeped in spirituality and the need for spiritual practices for people to discern the calling and will of God in their lives. A Native American approach to spiritual living gives a new means of accomplishing this sacred task.

So, what is spirituality from a Native American perspective? Early colonists would likely describe it using adjectives such as "savage," "evil," "satanic," or even "unholy." The simple truth is that for the early settlers it was a way of communing with the Creator in a way never before seen. Had due respect been given, it would have changed the lives of the early colonists profoundly and allowed for a holier time to prevail instead of the evil that historically took place. When broken down, Native American spirituality bears many of the same traits Christians have traditionally come to love and appreciate. Michael Garrett and Michael Wilbur, in their work "Does the Worm Live in the Ground? Reflections on Native American Spirituality," find that Native American spirituality is described through the four basic cultural elements of *medicine,*

28. Irwin, "Themes in Native American Spirituality," 311.

29. Neafsey, *Sacred Voice Is Calling,* 62.

harmony, *relation*, and *vision*.[30] Based on these four cultural elements, practical implications for counseling are offered concerning greeting, hospitality, silence, space, eye contact, intention, and collaboration. These four elements will permeate the rest of this section as Mr. Garrett and Mr. Wilbur have uncovered four central and important aspects of Native American spirituality.

David Hodge and Gordon Limb tackle the difficult concepts of Native American oppression and the role of spirituality in the life of Native Americans. They claim that Native American peoples are oppressed and thus suffer from a multitude of health issues and risks. "Indeed, although the dominant secular narrative often ignores spirituality, or even frames it as pathological, spirituality plays a central role in health and wellness for many Native Americans."[31] The authors note that there is a distinction between tribal differences and intertribal similarities concerning spirituality and spiritual health. Mr. Hoge and Mr. Limb focus more on the intersecting points to broadly speak on the role spirituality plays in the life of a Native American. They identify several key factors of intersection and major points of recognition spiritually for Native peoples.

> The anthropological framework posits that the three dimensions of personality—effect, will, and cognition—can be supplemented by three dimensions of the spirit—communion, conscience, and intuition. Communion refers to one's relationship with the Transcendent (that is, the Creator, God, or some other type of Transcendent dimension). Conscience refers to a sense of right and wrong. Intuition refers to the ability to know—to come up with insights that bypass normal cognitive channels.[32]

These six components resonate deeply with a broad span of different tribes and Native American people. "The instrument's most prominent strength was its congruence with the common Native American practice of oral storytelling."[33] Overall the article is

30. Garrett and Wilbur, "Does the Worm Live," 194.

31. Hodge and Limb, "Native American Perspective," 122.

32. Hodge and Limb, "Native American Perspective," 124.

33. Hodge and Limb, "Native American Perspective," 126.

geared to the premise that spiritual living has a formidable role in the lives of oppressed Native American people. In many ways, this article echoes the claims that have been made by Richardson, Neafsey, Bonhoeffer, and Reiser. There is a clear theme of the need for spiritual living as a matter of healthy living in the lives of all people. Although Hodge and Limb's article only addresses this in the context of oppressed Native Americans, the concept can easily be broadened when placed in the conversation of various other authors that this is not a distinct concept for Native American peoples. All people are in dire need of spiritual living and connection with the divine to live healthier lives. There is also a central claim to the health that Native Americans find in their oppressed state due to spiritual living and the lack of health many non-oppressed people find due to their lack of spiritual living. This contrast only intensifies the concept of the need for spiritual living to live a healthier life. Another direct link that Hodge and Limb make is in noting the large role that storytelling plays in the lives of Native American people.[34] Storytelling stands in direct link with Bonhoeffer's understanding of proclamation. Both authors are emphasizing this aspect of sharing, whether gospel, creation stories, or heritage truths, and the role spirituality plays in this process. For Bonhoeffer, spiritual living is the foundation for going and carrying out the calling of proclamation. Hodge and Limb claim that Native American people reveal storytelling as a means of spiritual living. It can easily be argued that both are correct and are emphasizing different parts of the same message, that the art of telling "truth" as we see it is a spiritual practice and must be founded in a strong spiritual life.

Lee Irwin writes on the misconceptions of Native American spirituality and the need for social misconceptions to be addressed. Irwin writes, "They involve a real need on the part of non-Native people to recognize the intrinsic worth of Native spiritual beliefs and practices that are, in fact, not easily accessible."[35] For Irwin, these misconceptions are rooted in "the disturbing history of religious persecution and denial of Native religious rights, coupled

34. Hodge and Limb, "Native American Perspective," 124.
35. Irwin, "Themes in Native American Spirituality," 309.

with an often-irresponsible public exposure of beliefs or practices regarded as deeply held facets of individual and communal identity, have led to a sheltering of Native spirituality from the public eye."[36]

> Perhaps the word "spiritual" needs clarification. My own understanding of spirituality in this context is something more than simply practicing a particular religion. This word "religion" doesn't sit well either in such context, being as it is a post-enlightenment concept often rooted in a polarity between ideas of the "sacred and profane." Such a distinction is an artificial and non-helpful locus for understanding the primary foundations of Native spirituality. My own experience of the interactive spheres of Native communal life is that they have a relatedness through personal relationships that finds common expression in mutual, everyday concerns. Ceremonial activity or prayer or simply carrying out daily activities, driving a friend to work, or struggling for political rights, may engage individuals in aspects of "religious" concern. It is that connectedness to core values and deep beliefs that I mean by "spirituality"—a pervasive quality of life that develops out of authentic participation in values and real-life practices meant to connect members of a community with the deepest foundations of personal affirmation and identity. In this sense, spirituality is inseparable from any sphere of activity as long as it connects with affirmative values and sources of authentic commitment and genuineness of concern.[37]

There is a serious concern in Irwin's writing on the representation of Native Americans and the lack of voice from Native people.

Overall, spirituality is a difficult and tricky concept to nail down. Whether religiously connected or secular, Indian or Christian, the concept of spirituality revolves heavily around daily and intentional living in connection with a higher deity. For Native Americans, this has traditionally coincided deeply with traditional

36. Irwin, "Themes in Native American Spirituality," 309.
37. Irwin, "Themes in Native American Spirituality," 311.

tribal creation stories and a sense of a Creator. Christians echo this with biblical terminology emphasizing the historic Jewish traditions of spiritual living as they have been nuanced in light of Jesus Christ and church tradition over the centuries. Whether it be God or Creator, both Indians and Christians find commonality in the reality of an instinctive and inborn need to live in connection with both higher forces and in peace and harmony with those around us. Living spiritually is not a gift bestowed on certain individuals who are more spiritual than others, it is a gift to all created persons to live deeply with God. Even more important, it isn't "hocus pocus" magic that cures the soul's innermost longings and wailings of loneliness and despair. That pain can only be cured by the presence of the divine, and it is this spiritual longing for the divine's presence that beckons to be filled like the ancient tobacco pipe filled with smoke. This ancient longing has been present since the days of creation felt first by the great ancestors Adam and Eve as they found themselves outside of the garden, longing to return to that celestial place of living with God. The earliest Native Americans felt this same longing and it was this longing that drew them into a way of living centered on peace, balance, harmony, and strength. Christians gave name to this longing as our created spirit that yearns to constantly dance with the Holy Spirit in light of the love of God through Jesus Christ. This longing gives way to the sacred, the holy, the divine to commune with us in profound ways and for a way of living to take place that draws God into every aspect.

IV

The "Native" Mindset

Growing up Native was a fascinating time in my life I will forever cherish. In many ways, I am still growing up Native until the day that I go to be with Ababinili. My Chickasaw mother was never one to "do" things, but rather we acted out of who we are. "Being" Native didn't mean that we made our traditional dishes, but we made *pashofa* and *Indian tacos* because we are Native. There was always a clear distinction between "doing" Native and "being" Native. "Being" Native meant we didn't sit around and talk about being Native all the time; we are Native and that's where that stood. We learned Chickasaw and ate traditional foods not to "do" Native things, but we did them because that's who we were, and these were the sacred ways of our people. This concept can be hard to grasp for some. One way of thinking about it is this: the bear does not hibernate to "do" bear things, the bear hibernates because it is a bear and hibernation has a purpose and meaning in the life of a bear simply being a bear. Many Native Americans simply live the way we live. Our social structure, our spiritual practices, and our mindset may be different from others, but this is ingrained into who we are as they are passed down from our elders as it has been for centuries. This concept is crucial because it allows being Indian to draw deeper into every aspect of life in profound ways. Being Indian begins to influence how you think, feel, and see the world around you, as well as every other part of yourself. It permeates your being in a way that every action, thought, word, and feeling is enveloped like a warm blanket in being Indian. Although being Indian is a way of life for Indian people, the process of "being" can be more broadly employed. Just as Natives *are* Native, the question becomes what it would look like for Christians to embrace this concept. What if being Christian became less of a checklist of daily boxes and more of a way of simply being?

NATIVE "BEINGS" NOT NATIVE "DOINGS"

So, what does it mean to have a Native mindset for Native people? Richard Twiss understands Native American culture as a starting place for the Christian church, saying, "Native culture like all the cultures of man, reflect some degree the attributes of our Creator Himself. . . . We see God working in terms of Jewish culture to reach Jews yet refusing to impose Jewish customs on Gentiles. Instead, non-Jews are to come to God and relate to Him in terms of their cultural vehicles. We see the Bible endorsing, then, a doctrine we call biblical sociocultural adequacy in which each culture is taken seriously but none advocate exclusively as the only one acceptable to God."[1] Twiss's concept of all cultures having a divine value is crucial for future relations between Native Americans and broader society as well as for a "Native" mindset to be adopted within the Christian church as a new path emerges for spiritual living. This is a fundamental root for the Chickasaw people and many other tribes. "Chickasaw traditionalists believe one can never truly know oneself without innate knowledge of one's own culture—no matter what that culture may be. Cultural identity is the root of who we are. . . . A person cannot travel the journey of life without first understanding where he or she has come from or why he or she is moving forward."[2] "It can be difficult for non-Indian people to comprehend that for Indians brought up in their own people's

1. Twiss, *One Church, Many Tribes*, 62.
2. Cobb and Hogan, *Chickasaw*, 39.

traditions, history is more than a sequence of events objectively re-counted. History is the story of one's people's past. To be sure, but also the story of one's identity."[3] Henrietta Mann and Anita Phillips write that "human identity is an essential part of the wholeness of humanity. We might consider it an overarching principle that has its origins in the makeup of a person from birth, combined with and informed by the life experiences of that individual and by the groups to which the individual belongs."[4] The authors elaborate, saying, "For Native Americans, identity as tribal peoples born of a particular nation, clan, band or tribal town is also a primary part of who we are."[5] Joseph M. Marshall III describes the same thing from a Lakota perspective, stating, "Among us, the old ones are the best models for how we should live our lives. Every old person is a collection of stories because of all that each one has seen and lived and all that happens in the world around them in a lifetime."[6] Dennis H. McPherson and J. Douglas Rabb share in their book *Indian from the Inside: Native American Philosophy and Cultural Renewal* this same concept: "In the days of my grandparents, which ended very early in my childhood, I would spend hours listening to their stories of how they viewed the world. I vividly remember that buried in their tales was a prescription for dealing with the world as a place in which all beings were allowed the time and space to be themselves."[7] The degree of this Nativeness is dependent on many factors that include being born close to or far from tribal lands, adoption into non-Native families, intermarriage, and more. These factors influence to what extent this Indian identity is lived into. With these factors present, there is a great deal of Native Americans who are living on this Indian road or in this Indian way. "Walking our path each day involves claiming all that Creator God has poured into us as indigenous peoples. We think and act in ways that are substantially different from our brothers and sisters

3. Page, *In the Hands*, 17.

4. Mann and Phillips, *On This Spirit Walk*, 3.

5. Mann and Phillips, *On This Spirit Walk*, 5.

6. Marshall, *Lakota Way*, 1.

7. McPhearson and Rabb, *Indian from the Inside*, 24.

from other racial-ethnic groups."[8] The authors describe the Cheyenne welcoming ceremony where newborns are welcomed by an elder to the spirits of the four directions and a prayer is offered for the health and longevity of this infant.[9] The child is then passed around and held and cuddled by all present as a way of establishing the child's identity within the group. Further, the act of naming is equally as important and sacred. These names direct the flow of the Natives' lives and give them purpose and meaning in living up to this special name. Although the Indian schools often took these names and replaced them with Anglicized names to de-Native these children. "The very identity of these children was threatened personally, culturally, and spiritually. They were subjected harshly to a methodical break up of everything they were in terms of their ethnic identity, the effects of which can still be felt in the twenty-first century."[10] From birth and adolescence, the cultural teachings imparted to young Natives are crucial, and this formative period is unmatched when it comes to imparting a cultural identity unto the child. Mrs. Mann and Mrs. Phillips talk extensively about the role their ancestors played in shaping their identity and instilling in them a Native identity that has served them a lifetime. They write, "Every day we walk upon this earth we carry our value along with us. These values both shape us and simultaneously are shaped by us. We find that we hold unique, individual values which we experience as individual persons, and we also hold shared, group values which we experience as part of the large population(s) to which we belong."[11] They highlight the fact that Native American people have tribal affiliations that bring a distinct cultural identity as each tribe holds a unique cultural entity with its values, customs, and language.[12] Mrs. Mann and Mrs. Phillips do a wonderful job of illustrating this within this work as two different authors from two different tribes with very different customs and traditions.

8. Mann and Phillips, *On This Spirit Walk*, 3.

9. Mann and Phillips, *On This Spirit Walk*, 4.

10. Mann and Phillips, *On This Spirit Walk*, 5–6.

11. Mann and Phillips, *On This Spirit Walk*, 13.

12. Mann and Phillips, *On This Spirit Walk*, 13.

Where there are so many differences, at the same time they share so many commonalities. Being "Native" is not a blanket term for all Native Americans sharing similar customs and traditions, it is a term of how the values, customs, traditions, and ways of living are instilled in Natives from a very young age. These values, concepts, customs, and ways of life can influence every aspect of Indian life and become so incorporated that they permeate the very being of a person undergirding all that they say, think, and do. Denise Linn contributes to this conversation by sharing her experience with the Maori tribe of New Zealand as well as the wise words of an Aborigine teacher about being "Native," saying, "It's not what is in your blood, but what is in your soul."[13] Truer words may have never been spoken. The author's experience centers on the aspects of "being" Native instead of "doing" Native as the core values and principles broadly shared within Native American communities are instilled to a degree that they permeate every facet of a person's life. Historic Chickasaw governor Overton James is credited with saying, "I do think there are things about the Indian way that are worth keeping. We have not traditionally been obsessed with material gain, and we haven't been prisoners of time schedules. I think those are good."[14] For Mrs. Mann and Mrs. Philips, these values are often contrary to what normal society values or embodies. The authors go as far as to compare the congruent values within many to most Native American tribes to the major cultural values found in American society.

13. Linn, *Kindling the Native Spirit*, xxiv.
14. Milligan, *Indian Way: Chickasaws*, 9.

VALUES COMPARISON CHART

Below is a list of contrasts that demonstrate why many American Indians find it difficult to achieve a balance between their values of the dominant society.

American Indian Values	Majority Culture American Values
Value the person	Value a person's possessions
Great respect for elders	Idealizing youthfulness
Sharing of material goods	Private ownership
Humility	Competitiveness
Honoring past traditions	Future orientation/planning
Emphasize the mystical	Emphasize the scientific
Harmony with nature	Dominating nature
Community cooperation	Individualism/Independence

Although these comparisons may seem dramatic and some may even argue against them, they strongly reflect the perception Native Americans have of America's predominantly non-Native society. [15] James Treat in his book *Native and Christian* would agree with this list as he writes, "The spirituality of Native American peoples developed for thousands of years within the context of the tribe before any contact with non-Indian's religions. There was also considerable interaction and dialogue among tribes about spiritual concepts. For instance, most tribes had a tradition of what could be compared to the law of reciprocal hospitality in the tribal history of the Hebrew people."[16] Taiaiake Alfred and Jeff Corntassel argue alongside Mr. Treat and Mrs. Mann and Mrs. Phillips in saying that this Native identity is best understood in light of the contemporary colonialism of today's society. They write, "Indigenousness is an identity constructed, shaped, and lived in the politicized context of contemporary colonials. The communities, clans, nations, and tribes we call Indigenous peoples are just that: Indigenous to the lands they inhabit, in contrast to and in contention with the colonial societies and states that have spread out from

15. Mann and Phillips, *On This Spirit Walk*, 17.
16. Treat, *Native and Christian*, 31.

Europe and other centers of the empire."[17] Among the wonderful examples they offer is of Canadian Natives that have embraced the government's label of "aboriginal," creating an identity that is colonial-minded and motivated as it works to incorporate Indigenous identity into the framework of Canadian culture while undermining the terrestrial claims the Indigenous people have.[18] In many regards, the ideas and motivations of the early colonists can still be interwoven into society today as much as it was centuries ago when first contact took place. Mrs. Mann and Mrs. Phillips go on to argue that the values of Native American communities, those shared and common values that are seen intertribally, are values that can biblically be found as the core values of the earliest Christian community.[19] This simple and yet complex aspect of terminology is a small example of the many ploys against Native Americans. Here "Nativeness" reveals even deeper degrees the presence of and power of a Native mentality within society today despite the ongoing forces to rid the world of the Native presence. These forces give a deeper claim to what it means to be Native. Mrs. Mann and Mrs. Phillips draw upon the testimony of George Catlin who writes, "I have visited 48 different tribes of the Great Plains, and feel authorized to say that the North American Indian in his native state is honest, hospitable, faithful, brave, and an honorable and religious human being."[20] These are the values and core concepts of what it means to be "Native." These values and ways of life pervade a person's life to the point that these ways become involuntary in all that they do, say, and think.

Denise Linn writes, "There's immense value in igniting your native spirit because when you do, your intuition expands exponentially. Gateways to spiritual realms open, and life-force energy fills you."[21] This work is complemented by the work of Cherokee/Creek scholar Tom Holm who understands the concept of

17. Alfred and Corntassel, "Being Indigenous," 597.

18. Alfred and Corntassel, "Being Indigenous," 597.

19. Mann and Phillips, *On This Spirit Walk*, 18.

20. Mann and Phillips, *On This Spirit Walk*, 18.

21. Linn, *Kindling the Native Spirit*, xxiv.

peoplehood as "four interlocking concepts: sacred history, ceremonial cycles, language, and ancestral homelands."[22] The cautionary note here is that being "Native" is a way of life for Native Americans. As we have seen in the previous chapter, the harm done with cheap and false representations of Native American ways of life have created more harm than imaginable for Native American people. The commercialization of Indian ways, traditions, and cultures must cease in American society. It is the concept of "being" instead of "doing" that this chapter focuses on highlighting. As Doug Goodfeather writes,

> There's a fine line between the appreciation of culture and the appropriation of that culture. To appropriate a culture means to emulate and imitate the distinct language, music, designs, symbols, rituals, traditions, mannerisms, and styles of dress that make up the defining elements of a specific group of people and their heritage. When someone who is not of a specific heritage steals any element of that culture, they are insulting and dishonoring the great love and loss, victories and defeats, and joys and suffering that were experienced and endured to achieve that distinct heritage and become that unique cultural identity.[23]

Mr. Goodfeather articulates the nuances of the Red Road and an understanding of being "In a Good Way" as Native American terms for those who embody the universal truths and sacred principles of Native American peoples over the centuries and whose actions are in alignment with such principles and truths.[24] This resonates deeply with the concepts of "being" versus "doing." To be on the Red Road, a person must be in a state of being instead of simply doing the acts of this way. For Kaitlin B. Curtice in her book *Native: Identity, Belonging, and Rediscovering God*, being Indigenous is a way of remembering, a way of carrying stories within us that

22. Alfred and Corntassel, "Being Indigenous," 609.

23. Goodfeather, *Think Indigenous*, 7.

24. Goodfeather, *Think Indigenous*, 7–8.

influence and guide us on our life's journey.[25] She points to the Native way as a way of remembering who we are and who we have been; a way of journeying and perseverance; a way of honoring creation and the great creation itself; it is a way that sees equality for all and denounces white supremacy; it is a way of speaking love and living a heart language; it is a way prayer, struggle, honoring ancestors; a way that sees all people and paves a way for the future that is far brighter than we ever imagined. Another way of looking at it is this, if a person is simply doing the acts and is not being this sacred way, these acts will fall short as the person's conflicting identities will eventually reveal themselves in often ugly ways. A person that is "being" will have no conflict about who they are and what they do because being "In a Good Way" will be natural and will derive out of the innermost recesses of that person's soul. Where this sounds wonderful and possibly even easily attainable, the reality is that the Christian church mindset and the Native American mindset are not so easily miscible. In his article "Canaanites, Cowboys, and Indians: Deliverance, Conquest, and Liberation Theology Today," Robert Allen Warrior writes, "It sounds like the perfect marriage—Christians with the desire to include Native Americans in their struggle for justice and Indian activists in need of resources and support from non-Indians. Well, speaking as the product of a marriage between an Indian and a white, I can tell you that it is not as easy as it sounds."[26] This challenging reality is both a testament to who Native Americans have had to become over the years and a sad reminder of the lack of embrace Indigenous people have found which has led to a strong sense of cultural resilience. In many ways, cultural resilience is a hallmark of what it means to be Native. Iris HeavyRunner (Blackfeet) and Joann Sebastian Morris (Sault Ste. Marie Chippewa) write, "Cultural resilience is a relatively new term, but it is a concept that predates the so-called 'discovery' of our people. The elders teach us that our children are gifts from the Creator, and it is the family, community, school, and tribe's responsibility to nurture, protect, and guide them. We have

25. Curtice, *Native*, 5.
26. Warrior, "Canaanites, Cowboys, and Indians," 21.

long recognized how important it is for children to have people in their lives who nurture their spirit, stand by, encourage and support them."[27] The two authors highlight the central aspects of Native American spirituality by saying, "Spirituality is a fundamental, continuous part of our lives. In traditional times, spirituality was integral to one's daily life. Embodied in Native spirituality is the concept of interconnectedness. The spiritual nature of all living things was recognized and respected."[28]

"Being" and "doing" are two very different things. To do something is an action, to be something is an adjective. For true doing to occur that is authentic and natural, a deep sense of being must first be found. This requires work! It requires commitment and letting go of who we are so that we might become all that we were created to be. "Being" demands listening to our ancestors and letting their voices guide our footsteps. "Being" requires us to know our past, present, and future and to always live in balance of these three. "Being" needs us to learn and know our sacred ways of living and the traditions that make us who we are so that we can continue them and teach them so that they are never lost. "Being" is a total commitment of our entire selves to be transformed and molded by a way of life more ancient than we can imagine and more sacred than we ever dreamed.

CHRISTIAN "BEINGS" NOT CHRISTIAN "DOINGS"

"As we pass through the many stages of life, our Christian faith informs and shapes our decisions, career, relationships, and all the other components that make up our identity."[29]

Now that a concept of "being" versus "doing" and the important role it plays in Native American communities has been established, the question that remains is whether there is room for this same concept to be applied to the Christian community. For

---

27. HeavyRunner and Morris, "Traditional Native Culture," para. 1.

28. HeavyRunner and Morris, "Traditional Native Culture," para. 4.

29. Mann and Phillips, *On This Spirit Walk*, 3.

Indian peoples, it is a natural way of life that the culture, traditions, and ways of life be passed on at an early age in a way that they become such an integral part of who we are that everything stems from this sacred place. The logo of the Chickasaw Cultural Center is a testament to this in so many ways. The three symbols of the spiral, the eye, and the sun, which are all connected, represent the Chickasaw way of life.

The logo begins with a spiritual representative of the wind, which connects with the *ogee* (eye), finally connecting with the sun. The connecting strand that runs through the emblem is important as it represents the connection between all three of the symbols as one way of living in connection with Ababinili. The spiral symbolizes wind, which is symbolic of each person's passage from birth, through life, and into the afterlife.[30] The *ogee*, or "all-seeing eye," embodies how our people view the world around us.[31] The sun stands for rebirth, the heavens, and the giver of light as it provides light and warmth to the world. In visual form, these symbols embody the way of the Chickasaw and represent so much that we hold sacred and dear in our lives.[32] These symbols act as guiding lights on our pathway in this life to be who Ababinili (Creator) created us to be. Just as these symbols guide the way of the Chickasaw people, so does the cross guide the way of Christian people.

Henrietta Mann and Anita Phillips speak to this very concept by saying, "For Christians, identifying as followers of Jesus Christ is a primary part of who we are. We strive to live out our lives as disciples according to this identity."[33] The emphasis is on the "being" instead of the simple and surface-level acts of "doing." Daniel Ang wonderfully articulates this concept in stating, "The sacramental life, therefore, calls for a life of faith which develops deep roots, a genuine spirituality, for the essence of Christian life is not a particular method or practice by a living encounter with a

30. "Heartbeat of a Nation."
31. "Heartbeat of a Nation."
32. "Heartbeat of A Nation."
33. Mann and Phillips, *On This Spirit Walk*, 3.

person and a community of believers."[34] The identity found in baptism speaks to the identity found in God through Jesus Christ by the power of the Holy Spirit. Kaitlin B. Curtice ponders this same point: "What if our stories of baptism in the church were rooted in that same idea of new beginnings, of personhood, just like the new beginning after a flood, after everything is drenched and overcome? What might we learn from the water? What might we learn if we listen, if we wade in—unafraid, untethered, and uninhibited—ready to become the ones we were created to become?"[35] In the baptismal liturgy of the United Methodist Church, and similarly, in many other denominations, we renounce forces of evil and wickedness, accept the freedom and grace of God to live beyond sin, and confess Christ as our Lord and Savior. For many in their adult lives, they have had an entire childhood of upbringing helping them learn and see what they are saying "yes" to in their baptism. Much like the adolescent rituals found in Native American communities, young Christians too find themselves enveloped in catechism from the earliest of ages. The parallels here are easily visible, but the question posed by Mrs. Curtice is breathtakingly deeper. For Mrs. Curtice, the question is this: How clear is the new identity and personhood baptizees receive from Christ in their baptism? The ecclesial challenge Mrs. Curtice proposes is one of serious consideration. For many, the act of being baptized is more of a "doing" than a "being," and this is precisely the argument that is being made. If the sacred act of baptism is being seen as more of a "doing" than a "being," there is a fundamental breakdown theologically and sacramentally. This breakdown can be attributed to many different reasons. Some might argue that the fast-paced consumer society of today lends for a theological interpretation of baptism as more of a transactional event instead of a lifelong commitment and change of personhood. Others might argue that certain theological influences are still in existence that lend to a "once saved always saved" mentality of baptism. Even yet, others might argue that the overly commercialized and satirized habits of

34. Ang, "Diminishing Mass Attendance," 23.
35. Curtice, *Native*, 11.

today's time lend to a surface-level baptismal theology that negates the true depths of baptismal identity altogether. In the struggling climate of the church today, it can easily be argued that no matter what the reasons are, there is a serious disconnect within the global church and the understanding of baptism. If baptism, as Mrs. Curtice and so many others argue, is the acceptance of an inherited identity that creates a new person and new beginning altogether, why the lapse found in the church today?

For a sense of "being" to be adopted in the Christian faith as it occurs in the Native American community, a sense of calling must first be addressed. For John Neafsey, love stands at the center of this conversation. Mr. Neafsey writes in *A Sacred Voice Is Calling: Personal Vocation and Social Conscience* that the precise point of love must be at the root of all that we do as Christian believers and this is not only a commandment of our Lord and Savior but is a calling that exists upon all who believe.[36] When love is the motivating factor in our lives, our most authentic and most sacred calling is answered, and our lives become a beautiful expression of the love and grace of God manifested in the life, death, and resurrection of Jesus Christ. Mr. Neafsey focuses on the aspect of letting love become who we are, our "being," which is much more than what we do, our "doing." To do love would be an empty, passionless action that the world sees over and over daily. To be loving is a way of life where love is manifested in genuine ways constantly. Mr. Neafsey focuses on several significant points that serve as the foundation to this calling as the acts of hearing, discerning, and responding. It is through personal vocation, social consciousness, listening, understanding the heart, creating an authentic expression, uplifting passion, compassion, visioning, suffering, and understanding conscience that this sacred calling is lived out. At the heart of hearing, discerning, and responding to this sacred calling is a love of learning and learning to love, hearing the cry of the needy and responding in love, and an authentic reaction that refuses imitation but resonates with the love of the saints. "Ultimately, however, we are not called to imitate the patterns of holiness that others have

36. Neafsey, *Sacred Voice Is Calling*, 3.

provided for us, however noble and beautiful these may be. Rather, we are called to discover our patterns, our unique personal path to holiness."[37] At the heart of hearing, discerning, and responding to this sacred calling is a love of learning and learning to love, hearing the cry of the needy and responding in love, and an authentic reaction that refuses imitation but resonates with the love of the saints. This is our sacred calling; this is love living and breathing in the world today.

From a scriptural standpoint, there is a great precedent for this calling and change of "being" in our relationship with God through Jesus Christ with the power of the Holy Spirit. The Old Testament is full of references to be a Christian "being" instead of a Christian "doing." From the words of God to Adam and Eve to go and fill the earth to Abraham promised generations as numerous as the stars, there is a clear understanding of God's people. Deuteronomy 7:6 identifies God's people in saying, "For you are a holy people to the Lord your God; the Lord your God has chosen you to be a people for His own possession out of all the peoples who are on the face of the earth" (ESV). God clearly identifies those who believe and follow God as a people of God, who are to be "holy men to Me, therefore you shall not eat any flesh torn to pieces in the field; you shall throw it to the dogs" (Exod 22:31 NKJV). Not only has God established who God's people are, but there is a clear understanding of what these people are and are not supposed to do. This can further be seen in the book of Leviticus with the Levitical codes that govern the people of God and guide their every action. "For I am the Lord your God. Consecrate yourselves, therefore, and be holy, for I am holy. And you shall not make yourselves unclean with any of the swarming things that swarm on the earth. For I am the Lord who brought you up from the land of Egypt to be your God; thus, you shall be holy, for I am holy" (Lev 11:44–45 ESV). Although the ancient Israelites struggled with this concept and went back and forth in their obedience, from the earliest Scriptures of the Bible a clear calling is made for God's people to live a certain way that is both distinguishable and

37. Neafsey, *Sacred Voice Is Calling*, 56.

identifiable from others. Proverbs takes things much deeper as the book calls for God's people to "speak up for those who cannot speak for themselves, for the rights of all who are destitute. Speak up and judge fairly; defend the rights of the poor and needy" (Prov 31:8–9). This calling to uphold righteousness and goodness even when it is difficult is central to the same calling that the prophets have concerning "being" a Christian and not just simply "doing" Christianity.

The voices of the prophets echo this message and double down on its importance as the Israelites struggle greatly with what it means to live for God and not for the world. Isaiah's words amplify this message as he encourages, "And they will call them, 'The holy people, The redeemed of the Lord'; And you will be called, 'Sought out, a city not forsaken'" (Isa 62:12 NKJV). Isaiah is not done there; the prophet goes on to what this calling entails, saying, "Learn to do right; seek justice. Defend the oppressed. Take up the cause of the fatherless; plead the case of the widow" (Isa 1:17). The term "holy" is important in the prophets' writings as it denotes an entire self-giving to God in deep and profound ways. To be holy was to be given to God for God's use and emblematic of the pureness of God. For God's people to live holy lives, as Isaiah and other writers are clearly articulating, God's people must live lives that God sees as good and pure. "Is not this the kind of fasting I have chosen: to lose the chains of injustice and untie the cords of the yoke, to set the oppressed free and break every yoke? Is it not to share your food with the hungry and to provide the poor wanderer with shelter—when you see the naked, to clothe them, and not to turn away from your own flesh and blood?" (Isa 58:6–7). The prophet Micah draws on the personal spirituality involved in this "being," saying, "He has shown you, O mortal, what is good. And what does the Lord require of you? To act justly and to love mercy and to walk humbly with your God" (Mic 6:8). The prophet Amos draws upon this word and adds, "Take away from Me the noise of your songs! I will not listen to the music of your harps. But let justice roll on like a river, and righteousness like an ever-flowing stream" (Amos 5:23–24 BSB). The prophets all point to a calling from God not just to be God's people, but to be God's people in the deepest sense of the word "be." This goes far deeper than simply doing. The prophets' take on this "being" is reflective in the world around the Israelite people. When justice rolls down like water, when justice and mercy are evident because of this walking with God, when those in need have their needs met, this is when "being" a Christian takes place. When the gospel permeates so deeply into a person's soul and every being that everything is drawn from this place is when Christian "being" takes place and true disciples of Jesus Christ are born.

The early apostles of Jesus are the greatest example we have of human "beings." Not only are they ideal because they reveal the human struggle involved with being a follower of Jesus, but they reveal the true change that happens when a person allows themselves to truly commit and become a Christian "being" and much more than a simple "doer" of Christianity. A "doer" gets to hold on to their old way of life while "doing" things that seem and appear as if they are truly Christian. Famed theologian and writer Dietrich Bonhoeffer thought the same:

> Cheap grace means grace sold on the market like cheap jacks' wares. The sacraments, the forgiveness of sin, and the consolations of religion are thrown away at cut prices. Grace is represented as the Church's inexhaustible treasury, from which she showers blessings with generous hands, without asking questions or fixing limits. Grace without price; grace without cost! The essence of grace, we suppose, is that the account has been paid in advance; and, because it has been paid, everything can be had for nothing. Since the cost was infinite, the possibilities of using and spending it are infinite. What would grace be if it were not cheap? Cheap grace is the preaching of forgiveness without requiring repentance, baptism without church discipline, Communion without confession, absolution without personal confession. Cheap grace is grace without discipleship, grace without the cross, grace without Jesus Christ, living and incarnate. Costly grace is the treasure hidden in the field; for the sake of it, a man will go and sell all that he has. It is the pearl of great

price to buy which the merchant will sell all his goods. It is the kingly rule of Christ, for whose sake a man will pluck out the eye which causes him to stumble; it is the call of Jesus Christ at which the disciple leaves his nets and follows him. Costly grace is the gospel which must be sought again and again, the gift which must be asked for, the door at which a man must knock. Such grace is costly because it calls us to follow, and it is grace because it calls us to follow Jesus Christ. It is costly because it costs a man his life, and it is grace because it gives a man the only true life. It is costly because it condemns sin, and grace because it justifies the sinner. Above all, it is costly because it cost God the life of his Son: "ye were bought at a price," and what has cost God much cannot be cheap for us. Above all, it is grace because God did not reckon his Son too dear a price to pay for our life but delivered Him up for us. Costly grace is the Incarnation of God.[38]

The passion and vigor in which Mr. Bonhoeffer approaches this topic is unparalleled and his words ring out in the Christian church today. The concept of "being" a Christian and not just simply "doing" Christian acts has been around since the time of Jesus Christ. It's the very reason that God incarnate came in the form of Jesus Christ. People have been struggling with the concept of "being" Christians for ages and will likely continue until God brings all things into fruition. Nevertheless, there is always hope and a fighting chance that change will take place. The history of Christendom is full of wonderful examples of saints that have exemplified what true "being" has looked like. Mother Theresa of Calcutta, Martin Luther King Jr., John of the Cross, and so many more have lived their lives so enveloped and impacted by the gospel that it began to be part of every aspect of their lives. Matthew 16:24 makes this clear when Jesus told his disciples, "If anyone would come after me, let him deny himself and take up his cross and follow me" (ESV). Another great Matthean view of this sense of "being" comes from Matt 6:33–34: "But seek first his kingdom and his righteousness, and all these things will be given to you as well. Therefore, do not

38. Bonhoeffer, *Cost of Discipleship*, 44.

worry about tomorrow, for tomorrow will worry about itself. Each day has enough trouble of its own." Paul also has a voice in this conversation as one of the prolific writers in the Christian tradition. His many epistles to the various churches give guidance and direction to young Christian communities struggling to get started and get going in the wake of the risen Christ. "Nevertheless, each person should live as a believer in whatever situation the Lord has assigned to them, just as God has called them. This is the rule I lay down in all the churches" (1 Cor 7:17). Similarly, to the church in Ephesus he writes, "As a prisoner for the Lord, then, I urge you to live a life worthy of the calling you have received. Be completely humble and gentle; be patient, bearing with one another in love. Make every effort to keep the unity of the Spirit through the bond of peace. There is one body and one Spirit, just as you were called to one hope when you were called; one Lord, one faith, one baptism; one God and Father of all, who is over all and through all and in all" (Eph 4:1–6). Another great examples of his emphasis on the selfishness of Christian living can be found in his letter to the church in Philippi, where he writes, "Therefore if you have any encouragement from being united with Christ, if any comfort from his love, if any common sharing in the Spirit, if any tenderness and compassion, then make my joy complete by being like-minded, having the same love, being one in spirit and of one mind. Do nothing out of selfish ambition or vain conceit. Rather, in humility value others above yourselves, not looking to your own interests but each of you to the interests of the others" (Phil 2:1–4). Paul goes on in his second letter to Timothy and states, "He has saved us and called us to a holy life—not because of anything we have done but because of his own purpose and grace" (2 Tim 1:10). Paul even draws on a common thread of ancestral presence in his Hebrew letter, where he speaks of the great cloud of witnesses. "Therefore, since we are surrounded by such a great cloud of witnesses, let us throw off everything that hinders and the sin that so easily entangles" (Heb 12:1–2). There is a great parallel here with the Native American concept of ancestry and the Christian understanding of ancestry where both communities embrace the presence of ancestors as guiding lights on the pathway of life. Paul draws upon the relational value of this "being" in his letter to Peter, where he states, "Each of you should use whatever gift you have received to serve others, as faithful stewards of God's grace in its various forms" (1 Pet 4:10–11). This "being" should consume us to the point that we freely give and care for those around us as love takes the forefront of every part of our being.

"Being" and "doing" are two words that bear a great deal of weight and meaning. Native Americans have come to know and recognize those around them that simply "do" Native American practices and adorn Indian designed clothing and apparel from those who live into "being" Native American where their entire lives are driven by a sense of purpose, belonging, and set of standards and beliefs. Simple "doers" of Native American culture perpetuate harmful gimmicks that ultimately harm the Native American community even further than it already has been. For those that live into "being" Native, our lives are constantly being fueled by a deep sense of ancient beliefs, traditions, and ways of life that are not customary or typical in modern society in most cases. These ancient ways of love, sacrifice, service, dignity, humility, and perseverance are taught and awakened at the earliest ages and are instilled in us from the earliest point possible. Likewise, the Christian community needs more Christian "being" and less Christian "doing." Believers today have come to a place of complacency and simplicity in their faith that is leading to a downturn in attendance and a lack of authentic and genuine faith. For so many people, the act of attending worship services, regular tithing, and occasional spiritual practices are enough to claim the title of Christian with little to no change or new creation. Many would argue the Christian church is struggling today not with occupancy, but with authenticity. The lack of authentic and genuine discipleship that the Old Testament demanded God's people turn from, that Jesus Christ pleaded for all who believe in him to repent of, and that Paul tirelessly appealed in his writings for the church to move past. For a Native American way of spirituality to influence the church, the starting point must be with authentic living. Cheap gimmicks of spirituality are plaguing the church and for true and deep spiritual renewal to take root, the ground must first be tilled. The foundation must first be weeded, and old ways of simple and surface level faith must be overcome with a deep sense of "being." Joseph Epes Brown emphasizes the role Native American spirituality has to offer a struggling and dying Christian church in saying, "For centuries the American Indian peoples have been involved in a struggle that has taken on the proportions of a tragedy. It is a double tragedy, for it is ours as well as their, and it is still being enacted today. These original Americans have had, and fortunately still do have, great riches in human spiritual resources. Yet these riches are either being swept aside and forgotten or are being consciously and actively destroyed by a civilization that is out of balance precisely because it has lost those values."[39] It is when, and if, the Christian church can begin to appreciate, respect, and revere the Native American people and Native ways of life that a new path to spiritual living with God can arise.

39. Brown, *Spiritual Legacy*, 21.

V

In Need of a New Way

John Wesley, the founder of the Methodist movement that led to the Methodist denomination, passionately and fearfully said these words towards the end of his life, "I am not afraid that the people called Methodists should ever cease to exist either in Europe or America. But I am afraid lest they should only exist as a dead sect, having the form of religion without the power. And this undoubtedly will be the case unless they hold fast both the doctrine, spirit, and discipline with which they first set out."[1] In many ways the fears of Mr. Wesley have sadly come to fruition as the Christian church has seen a decline over the past few decades that question whether it will ever be able to recover. One of the areas that the church has struggled with over ages is a concept of spirituality that often feels outdated and as historic as its pioneers. There are many different versions of ancient forms of spirituality within the Christian tradition that all offer a unique way of communing with God in daily life. These ancient and traditional forms of spiritual living all offer so much to the spiritual landscape and are tested and found to be true by the Christian church over the centuries. The trouble is in no way with these historic forms of spiritual living; in fact, they are in every way effective and deeply

1. Wesley, *Journal of John Wesley*, 362.

useful resources when it comes to living spiritually. They serve as a wonderful foundation for the continued work and exploration of spirituality to take place. The issue arises in the fact that the Christian church has been using these ancient forms of spiritual living and the language that is specific to their various forms for centuries with little to no innovation. When met with a consumer society that is as fast paced and constantly seeking new and fresh expressions, the conflict is easy to see. Christians today want a fresh approach to spiritual living that explores avenues of spirituality that these ancient forms rarely if at all touch. Although in a fundamental sense these ancient practices are treasures and for any Christian should be rightfully and duly explored, there is great demand for a new way of spiritual living to emerge that encompasses a fresh approach to spiritual living.

EVER ANCIENT, EVER NEW

Due appreciation needs to be given to the ancient practices of the Christian church before a conversation can take place regarding the need for new expression. The reality is that these practices, ancient as they may be, have time-tested effectiveness in guiding persons to a deeper spiritual life with God. The Roman Catholic Church has many orders that stand as pillars in shaping and forming the spiritual landscape over the past several centuries. These sacred ways of living in deep communion with God need no introduction for many Christians today and are well versed in the spiritual landscape that Christians in the twenty-first century find themselves in. Serving as a foundation for the new paths of spirituality to emerge, these sacred ways are the fertile ground from which all new expressions can spring forth.

The spiritual practice of preaching has been around as a communal way of connecting with God since biblical times. The first preacher to proclaim the good news of the risen Jesus Christ was Mary Magdalene, running to tell the disciples of what she had witnessed and that the Lord had risen. Although Mary is the first New Testament preacher to preach the gospel, the Old Testament is full of prophets and saints proclaiming the good news of God's love and the need for obedience. Even theologian Dietrich Bonhoeffer knew of the power of proclamation as a spiritual avenue. For Bonhoeffer, spiritual care is rooted in the theological principle of the love of God. To proclaim the Lord is to proclaim love. Proclamation is ministering to people in need, and this is divine. It is a gift from God to humanity. Thus, proclamation is to provide that God is our help and comforter, but also Christ in his victory is a victory over sickness, death, pain, and suffering, and that forgiveness was provided on the cross. This proclamation is the mission of spiritual care, which is the mission and ministry to proclaim the word, both of which Bonhoeffer sees as being linked.[2] The Dominican Order, also known as the Order of Preachers, emphasizes the theological and spiritual aspects of preaching as a direct and unique way of communing with God. For members of the Dominican Order, preaching is a direct way of living in deep spiritual connection with the Creator.[3]

St. Francis of Assisi may very well be one of the most common and recognizable names in Roman Catholicism as well as Christian spiritualism. Known for his life of poverty and rule of *Regula primitiva* ("Primitive Rule"), St. Francis founded the Order of Lesser Brothers as those who lived a spiritual life emphasizing the way of Jesus Christ that centers on both poverty and fraternity.[4] Often referred to as the Joyful Beggar, St. Francis found a spiritual way of humbleness and simplicity that many rarely find in today's consumer-based society.

The Jesuits, founded by St. Ignatius of Loyola, pride themselves on a spiritual life focused on finding God in all things. Values universally found in Ignatian spirituality are core values fundamental to the gospel, such as authenticity, integrity, courage, love, forgiveness, hope, healing, service and justice.[5] In brief summary, the Ignatian way of spirituality emphasized the spiritual

2. Bonhoeffer, *Spiritual Care*, 48.

3. Currier, *History of Religious Orders*, 22.

4. Currier, *History of Religious Orders*, 18.

5. Currier, *History of Religious Orders*, 22.

exercises, prayer and contemplation, the Examen, and discernment. In many ways this fundamental approach has led thousands to a deeper relationship with God through Jesus Christ by the power of the Holy Spirit. Ignatian spirituality centers on prayer and regular practice of spiritual exercises that guide people into a deeper understanding and realization of how God is moving in and through their lives in incredible and often unrecognized ways.

The Benedictine Order, founded by St. Benedict of Nursia, is a monastic religious order that has high regard for spiritual living in and through the act and art of teaching. For Benedictines, teaching is the closest way of emulating Christ who as Rabbi came to teach the truths of God that had been lost and misunderstood by humanity over the centuries.[6] The reality is that teaching can take on many different forms both formal and informal. From Sunday schools and academia to friendly conversations and cultivating young minds in a person's own family, the art of teaching knows no bounds and is a deep way of finding and living in harmony with God. James gives great caution to this spiritual practice in saying, "Not many of you should become teachers, my brothers, because you know that we who teach will be judged more strictly" (Jas 3:1 ESV). Where teachers are held to a higher standard because teaching by example is the greatest form of teaching, the spiritual power of finding God in teaching is surely evident.

THE TWENTY-FIRST-CENTURY CHURCH

Where only a few examples are given here where there are many more, the reality is the church has a wonderful foundation for spiritual living guided by passionate and faithful saints that have gone before us, leaving behind the gift of spiritual living in unique and powerful ways. The question is, thus, if such powerful ways of spiritual living are so readily available, why is there such a decline and shift spiritually within the Christian church? Such questions are complex and multifaceted and have perplexed the church for

6 Currier, *History of Religious Orders*, 23.

centuries. The truth is that young adults are rejecting the modern church primarily because what was once flashy and new is now old and decrepit in the eyes of so many young people, and the need for new is stronger than ever.[7] One reason is that in today's fast paced and consumer-based world, a need for a fresh expression of what these historic models have found to be true is both wanted and needed yet in a new form. Another is that these traditional forms of spiritual living have been around for so long now, that where they are effective, Christians find them lacking innovation and presence in the current church dialog. "Many young people today are not interested in a church that provides a slightly different version of what the world can give them. If the church is just another vendor of service—not even a good one in some cases—what does it have that they cannot get elsewhere?"[8] *The Blackwell Companion to Christian Spirituality* makes this argument:

> Christian spirituality in the modern period is often seen as characterized by a decline in the mystical tradition and the spiritual disciplines and devotional practices of Christendom. . . . Throughout the past three centuries, the Christian spiritual impulse has been continuously dislocated and relocated, disoriented and reoriented, and reorganized by a series of intellectual, political, social, and moral challenges. . . . This mosaic of Christian spirituality pictures one of the fundamental realities of the modern experience: the shift away from univocality to multivocality brought about by the inclusion of previously excluded voices. Much of the traditional Christian spirituality passed down to modern people was that of the "approved" sort; only rarely did outside voices of challenge sneak through institutional structures. . . . The creative response of Christian people to construct spiritualities able to answer the challenges of modernity has never been lacking. Perhaps all that has been lacking is the imaginative vision of observers to notice and offer

---

7. Bevins, *Ever Ancient, Ever New*, 29.

8. Bevins, *Ever Ancient, Ever New*, 29.

definitions of contemporary Christian spirituality that
match its creative experimentation in practice.[9]

Mr. Holder brings to surface several interesting aspects of spirituality in the twenty-first century. Mr. Holder understands spirituality as the ability to creatively respond and construct answers to the challenges of modernity, a phenomenon that has never been lacking. For Mr. Holder, the element that has been scarce is the ability to see and name how this is taking place. Many might argue that Mr. Holder's argument holds little claim considering the ongoing decline in membership in recent church history. Another argument may be made that in a pandemic world where online church is king, how is Mr. Holder's concept of creative Christian spirituality being lived out, if it is at all? Where these questions surmise all sorts of theological, epistemological, and philosophical thoughts, it cannot be denied that the church is indeed suffering both a spiritual and attendance decline. Daniel Ang makes the bold assessment that "the reasons for low levels of attendance at Mass are various and many of them are familiar: the perceived irrelevance of the Church to contemporary life, the felt misuse of power and authority in the Church, problems with the parish priest, and the feeling that being a committed Catholic no longer requires attending Mass as frequently, or even at all."[10] Where Mr. Ang's position is pointed towards the Roman Catholic Church, a great argument could easily be made for the same justification of any other mainline denomination in the twenty-first century. He emphasizes the work of Neil Brown, who suggests that the lack of presence in Mass, or worship in this conversation, has led to an estrangement of sacramental worship due to the lack of community of faith and praxis that God calls the body to be.[11] Mr. Ang stresses the importance of sacramental theology and spirituality and that this often has an inauthentic taste that is driving people from the church instead of towards Jesus Christ. Mr. Ang argues that

9. Holder, *Blackwell Companion to Christian Spirituality*, 10.

10. Ang, "Diminishing Mass Attendance," 21.

11. Ang, "Diminishing Mass Attendance," 21.

this inauthenticity arises from a misconception of the church as a people motivated by justice, prayer, contemplation, faithful living, hope, and above all love.[12] Mr. Ang calls in David Tacey, who stresses that there is a dire need for a shift from preaching evangelism to an evangelistic model focused on listening to the alienated, marginalized, and the seemingly impassive.[13] Ultimately Mr. Ang argues that the recent decline in participation in the Catholic Church, and some may argue broader Christianity, confronts the body of Christ to more deeply search out and hear those who feel marginalized, oppressed, and spirituality drained as a means of evangelism and disciple making.[14] This new way of hearing the "other" is fundamental in what Mr. Ang is arguing needs to drive the Christian church into the rest of the twenty-first century and beyond. It is exactly this place that a Native American voice can be heard crying out in the wilderness as John's did so long ago bearing witness to the Messiah. Mr. Ang's work gives claim to the need to hear the oppressed and marginalized as a way of hearing God and allowing a new spiritual way to emerge that Indian people can grasp. Further, Mr. Ang's work draws much deeper when it is considered in the framework of the Christian church's deep need for evaluation and change, including spiritually, for the church to survive and once again thrive. What has been left is a spiritual landscape that is multifaceted, multi-traditional, and convoluted to say the least.

Dick Houtman and Stef Aupers in the article "The Spiritual Turn and the Decline of Tradition: The Spread of Post-Christian Spirituality in 14 Western Countries" reveal a great deal about the spiritual topography of today. The authors argue that "most participants in the spiritual milieu, it is generally argued, draw upon multiple traditions, styles, and ideas simultaneously, combining them into idiosyncratic packages. Spirituality is thus referred to as 'do-it-yourself religion.'"[15] The reality is that both Christian, re-

---

12. Ang, "Diminishing Mass Attendance," 23.

13. Ang, "Diminishing Mass Attendance," 23.

14. Ang, "Diminishing Mass Attendance," 24.

15. Houtman and Aupers, "Spiritual Turn," 305.

ligious, and secular members of this environment all agree on the fragmented and convoluted nature of modern spirituality.[16] Mr. Houtman and Mr. Aupers stress the deep desire for fresh expressions within the spiritual context of the current times. The authors highlight the diversity found in the current climate and the lack of concern for purity in praxis versus the palpable vibrancy found in coalescing traditions. Mr. Houtman and Mr. Aupers assert, "This, then, is the main tenant of post-Christian spirituality: the belief that in the deepest layers of the self the 'divine spark'—to borrow a term from ancient Gnosticism—is still smoldering, waiting to be stirred up, and succeed the socialized self."[17] The authors wrestle with the emerging language of detraditionalization versus the new age language of individualization as a result of the lack of regard for purity concerning spiritual praxis as a prime example of the deep longing for a new spiritual expression to emerge. Where some would call this process detraditionalization, new age spirituality simply refers to it as individualization and creatively problem-solving the issue of traditional spirituality and its decrepit perception. Richard Twiss might argue that this is emblematic of the theological syncretism that he highlights in his book *Rescuing the Gospel from the Cowboys: A Native American Expression of the Jesus Way*.[18] This blending or mixing is a trend that is not only happening spiritually but is happening in powerful ways theologically.

With a deeply rich and vivid tradition of spiritual living in various traditions and orders, the Christian church has so much to offer the larger spiritual world. These spiritual ways serve as the foundation for the work of Native American spirituality and align with Christian spirituality in an intersectionality that showcases the complimentary nature of the two. The decline in the church in recent years stands as a testament to the dire need for new spiritual traditions and ways to emerge, evident in the intermingled and multi-traditional spiritual landscape today that struggles with tensions between competing notions of detraditionalization versus

16. Houtman and Aupers, "Spiritual Turn," 306.

17. Houtman and Aupers, "Spiritual Turn," 306–307.

18. Twiss, *Rescuing the Gospel*, 28.

individualization. The Christian church has been and will always be a constantly evolving and ever-growing entity that strives to live into the image and example of God in Jesus Christ empowered by the Holy Spirit. This nature of the church calls forth for innovation and constant development for the sake of spiritual health and not the needy cravings of a consumer society that thrives on invention for the sake of invention. The spiritual growth needed today is one of authenticity and deep faith that treasures the ways of the past while finding respect and reverence in hearing the sacred voices of an Indigenous people who have so much to offer. The ways of old will become the ways of new as Native American spiritual traditions offer a new way forward in spiritual living and a possible new age for the church to embrace and commence.

VI

A New Path Emerges

With the Christian church in the state that it is in, it is precisely this point and place that Native American spirituality has so much to offer. A Native and Christian approach to spiritual living is a new way of living in communion with God in a way that other forms of spirituality are limited to. Every method or form of spiritual living has its limitations when left on its own, so it comes as no surprise that Native American spirituality comes as a compliment to the historic Christian forms of spiritual living. The sound of the drum, the songs of old, the smell of *pishofa* and fry bread, the gathered tribe, the sound of moccasin stomps, the jingles of bell skirts, and the rattles of turtle shells are a way of communing with God never fully experienced in the Christian church. The inspiration of these traditions and practices brings a fresh breath of spiritual living that can offer what other forms cannot. These spiritual ways include community gatherings and mindsets, harmony in all things, and sacred ceremonies to bless the community.[1] The Native American practices that are shared in some way between most if not all tribes are wonderful expressions of what a new form of spirituality can look like. As mentioned above, these must be approached with a respect and reverence that prohibits

1. "Spirituality: Community, Harmony, Ceremony."

misrepresentations and reproductions that harm the authenticity and sacredness of these ancient practices. It is the inspiration of these spiritual ways that will bring a new and fresh approach to spiritual living in the twenty-first century. The ways offered as a new path to spiritual living are ways that draw from the spirit of traditional Native American practices and ways of life. In no way do they work to recreate or appropriate the sacred practice of Indian people. Instead, the spirit of these practices can be shared in ways that pay homage to traditional Native American ways of life while remaining respectfully distant so as not to continue to perpetuate harm towards Indigenous peoples. It is also important to note that these approaches must begin with a full commitment to spiritual living by taking a deep sense of "being" and not a sense of "doing." To simply do these acts would be to undermine the entire notion and biblical calling of spiritual living in and of itself. This way of life must first and foremost be just that, a way of life. Half-hearted spirituality is a plague that the Christian church is already struggling with and is at the root of where this new expression of spiritual living offers change and a bright new future. In essence it is best said by Rev. David Wilson of the Choctaw nation: "The Creator gave Indian people many ways to worship Him, . . . and they are ALL good!"[2]

GOOD MEDICINE

For centuries Native American peoples have had deep connections with utilizing the gifts offered by creation to bring healing and wholeness. Native Americans have been able to tap into the healing and wholeness powers in natural elements in ways still unknown to many.[3] In the Chickasaw tradition, "*Alikchi* had distinct and complementary skills. Healers practiced spiritual and physical medicine. Herbalists shared their intuition and knowledge, treating the body with herbs and roots. The gift of healing

2. "Modern Indian Christians."
3. "Useful Plants."

was often passed down through many generations."[4] Nowadays the role of *alikchi* is what modernity would refer to as doctors. Robin Wall Kimmerer speaks to the profound presence natural elements have in Indian traditional way of life. The bounty of the earth was a resource not only treasured by Native Americans but utilized in powerful ways. In speaking of sweet grass, Mrs. Kimmerer writes, "In our language it is called *wwingaashk,* the sweet-smelling hair of Mother Earth. Breathe it in and you start to remember things you didn't know you'd forgotten."[5] Throughout her book she highlights how strawberries, pecans, witch hazel, water lilies, squash, roots, corn, and so many other edibles and herbs are used in powerful ways to heal, cure, and bring wholeness. The story of Mrs. Mose Burris tells of her work as a medicine woman and how she is remembered by "her singing and chanting as she blew into the medicine with a bamboo stirring stick."[6] Johnson Perry tells of his experience as a child, claiming, "He used herbs in treating us, and I remember how he cured me of scarlet fever when I was real small."[7] Mary Ella Russel tells of her grandmother, who "knew all about herbs, and we used to have home remedies for everything you can think of. We'd take a tea made from wild cherry bark for coughs. Bitterweed makes a good tea for a fever. Use the stalk and blossoms. Chiggerweed tea is a sure cure for headaches, and broom weed tea is fine for a flu, colds, fever, and it makes a good cough syrup. Sassafras tea is good for kidney trouble."[8] She goes on to tell of many more teas and remedies her grandmother and family would use.

The medicinal progress Native Americans had found prior to European contact fascinated early colonists to the point of believing it was magic. Porter Shimer says, "Scientists have determined that more than 200 plants widely used by Native Americans contain medicinal compounds. In fact, some of our most commonly

4. "Sacred People."

5. Kimmerer, *Braiding Sweetgrass,* ix.

6. Milligan, *Indian Way: Chickasaws,* 27.

7. Milligan, *Indian Way: Chickasaws,* 49.

8. Milligan, *Indian Way: Chickasaws,* 63.

used drugs contain active ingredients found in plants that Native Americans knew and used—the aspirin-like compounds in willow are a perfect example."[9] Mr. Shimer goes on: "But botanists, historians, and pharmacologists who have studied Native American healing point to clear evidence that the early Native Americans knew exactly what they were doing."[10] Shimer goes on to break down how different herbs, plants, fruits, and vegetables were used in healing ways by Indian peoples. Denise Linn understands this sacred tradition as an elemental one where the four elements (water, earth, fire, and air) are all around us and constantly calling to us. "Answering a call to the elements is simply a matter of taking time to be aware of them. . . . To answer the call of the Spirit of Water, simply be aware of the water that is within you and around you from rain, fog, and snow. Also, take note of the water you drink, bathe in, and ingest when eating fruits and vegetables."[11] This concept of stewardship is defined by Adele Alhberg Calhoun as "the voluntary and generous offering of God's gift of resources, time, talents, and treasure for the benefit and love of God and others."[12]

Herbal health is not a popular or very lucrative market today. From herbal remedies that can be swallowed as pills, found in powders, brewed as tea, applied to the skin as gels, lotions, or creams, and added to bath water to the ever-popular essential oils trend, the notions of using natural remedies for healing and wholeness purposes are wonderful. Incense and herbal/natural fragrances have also been known to reduce stress, bring calm and peace to people's lives, and allow for more relaxed spaces and lifestyles. Whether you go by a Scentsy, diffuser, or hanging eucalyptus in your shower, finding God in the bounties of Mother Earth is limitless. Using these natural resources to draw closer to God is as natural as anything else and it allows God to use all of our senses as we seek to live more deeply with our Creator.

9. Shimer, *Healing Secrets*, 45.
10. Shimer, *Healing Secrets*, 46.
11. Linn, *Kindling the Native Spirit*, 9.
12. Calhoun, *Spiritual Disciplines Handbook*, 11.

PRAYER

Prayer is one of the oldest and most fundamental ways of living spiritually. To be in communication with God is a holy and sacred privilege. From the earliest records, Native Americans have had a very keen understanding of the Creator typically paired with an origin story. From there flowed the natural act of communicating with the Creator. For Adele Ahlberg Calhoun, prayer is a relational term and requires both intentionality and consistency.[13] Ancient Jewish customs believed prayer began with intentional awareness of the presence of God and central to any prayer is the posture, both physical and inward posture of the heart. The numerous traditional forms of prayer are vast, including breath prayers, centering prayer, contemplative prayers, conversational prayers, fixed-hour prayers, inner-healing prayers, intercessory prayers, labyrinth prayers, listening prayers, liturgical prayers, lamentations, partner praying, Scripture praying, recollection praying, walking prayers, and welcoming prayers to name only a few. Dallas Willard emphasizes the conversational aspect in saying that "conversation, when it is truly a conversation, makes an indelible impression on our minds, and our consciousness of him remains vivid as we go our way."[14] Elaine Heath writes, "The Christian faith is all about a relationship of love, trust, and vulnerability, on God's part and on ours. Prayer is the essence of that relationship. It is more than speaking and listening, more than liturgy or silence. Prayers are the very breath of God, breathing life into us, opening us to who God is, to who we are, and to this world that God loves. The breath of God brings life, healing, renewal, comfort, challenges, and direction. Just as breathing is necessary for life in our physical bodies, prayer is necessary for spiritual life."[15] These powerful words give way to the true depth and power prayer can have when it is seen as more than a simple means to temporarily pacifying the soul and rather as a way of living in constant communication with

13. Calhoun, *Spiritual Disciplines Handbook*, 232.

14. Willard, *Spirit of the Disciplines*, 184.

15. Heath, *Five Means of Grace*, 5.

God. A healthy prayer life is a crucial part of any person's spiritual health and prayers along the Indian Road emphasize the need for intentionality and consistency that allows space to both hear and be heard.

Native Americans have a wealth of practice concerning prayers. "Prayer—the daily recognition of the Unseen and the Eternal—is our one inevitable duty."[16] Whether praying around the fire so the smoke lifts the prayers to the heavens, to prayer ticks, and to even prayer arrows, Indians have found prayer as unique as the DNA of a person. Another Native American concept to prayer is the use of feathers in symbolic fashion of the belief that the feather will carry the prayer to the heavens. Doug Goodfeather of the Lakota Tribe writes that to live into our own unique prayer life we must first "start by connecting with your authentic voice."[17] A person who prays is very different from a person whose entire life is founded upon prayer. According to Evan B. Howard, "you can have all the correct techniques, from the right words and meditation format to devotional gestures and deep emotional feelings. But if your spirit is not present, if there is a disconnect between the depth of your heart and the form of your prayer, it is not prayer."[18] Prayer should be a natural part of life that draws from the deepest parts of who we are, what we struggle with, what triumphs we have. As Jack Levison puts it, "I don't want you, as a child of God . . . thinking of prayer as one more obligation to cross off your list. Let prayer today be for you a deep sigh, a contented breath."[19] "It cannot be forced but flourishes in the soil of freedom and mutual commitment. The health and vitality of this relationship depend on clarity and frequency of communication."[20] To live a life of prayer in the deepest way possible, in the spirit of Native American praying, is to let prayer envelope your life entirely to the

16. Nerburn, *Wisdom of the Native Americans*, 91.

17. Goodfeather, *Think Indigenous*, 35.

18. Howard, *Guide to Christian Spiritual Formation*, 137.

19. Levison, *40 Days*, 40

20. Thompson, *Soul Feast*, 31.

point that your very soul is laid before God as you converse with Ababinili (Creator).

DANCING

One of the first images many people envision when thinking about Native American people are the wonderful and elaborate dances of our people. According to Tara Browner, "A pow-wow is an event where American Indians of all nations come together to celebrate their culture through the medium of music and dance."[21] Linford D. Fisher writes that "the most common collective ritual in Native communities was the feast or dance. . . . These community gatherings were held at regular times throughout the year—in the early spring, late summer, and during the winter—as well as when necessitated by internal or external events or activities—sickness, drought, war, death, or marriage."[22] From Stomp Dances and hoop dances to Sun Dances, Jingle Skirt Dances, and *Pishofa* Dances, the act of dancing is as historic and spiritual as anything else in Indian life. "When I go to that arena, for me it's like going to church. . . . I have no worries. I don't hurt," says Opal Gore of the Comanche nation.[23] One common tradition associated with dancing is the use of shell shakers. "These 'shell shakers' are used in social dances among the Cherokee, Muskogee, Seminole, Choctaw, and Chickasaw peoples."[24] From a Chickasaw perspective these *Loski' chalha'chi'* (turtle shell shakers) are filled with pebbles, which provide the rhythmic accompaniment to Chickasaw Stomp Dances and social songs.[25]

Even from the earliest times people have been dancing as a way of connecting with the Creator and celebrating the wonders of life. From a biblical precedent, David gives us direct insight

21. Browner, *Heartbeat of the People*, 1.

22. Fisher, *Indian Great Awakening*, 19.

23. "Still Dancing."

24. "Shell Shakers."

25. "Loski' chalha'chi."

into the joys of dancing for and with God. "And David danced before the Lord with all his might, wearing a priestly garment. So, David and all the people of Israel brought up the Ark of the Lord with shouts of joy and the blowing of rams' horns" (2 Sam 6:14–22 NLT). The act of dancing is not only deeply spiritual, but exceptionally healthy.

> Dance is a mind–body experience that increases blood supply to the brain, provides an outlet for releasing emotional expression, allows for creativity, and the socialization aspect lowers stress, depression, and loneliness. . . . So how does one maintain a lifelong program of physical activity? If individuals perceive a particular activity as "fun" and not "boring exercise," their intent to become engaged may no longer be an issue. Today, more than ever before, individuals seeking a viable form of sustained physical activity choose dance for more reasons than exercise alone.[26]

"Because dance can take many forms, be performed in a variety of settings, and does not necessarily require much expense or equipment, it might appeal to a wide range of individuals of all ages."[27] Although Native American dance styles and traditions should not be recreated or appropriated in any shape or form, the spirit of dancing itself is one that can draw people into a closer spiritual walk with God. The medical and spiritual benefits speak for themselves as to why Native Americans have revered this sacred practice through the centuries. To lose oneself in dance and find themselves alone with God is a wonderful and breathtaking experience all should find at least once in their lifetime.

DRUMS

A conversation about Native American dancing can't be had without speaking of its sister tradition of drumming.

26. Alpert, "Health Benefits of Dance," 155.

27. Keogh et al., "Physical Benefits of Dancing," 481.

> As you hear the sound of the drum rumbling low to the
> sharp, impassioned cries of the singers, the vibration
> moves through you like a storm that rises in the distance,
> building slowly in the azure sky, then unloading in a
> rhythmic yet gentle pounding of the soil. Anyone, Native
> or non-Native, who has ever had the opportunity to ex-
> perience the colors, movement, sounds, tastes, and smells
> of the powwow (a pan-traditional, ceremonial giving of
> thanks) understands the feeling that passes through you.
> It is different for every person, but if you really experi-
> ence the feeling, you know that it is a connection. For
> some, it is a matter of seeing old friends or making new
> ones. For some, it is the image of the dancers moving in
> seemingly infinite poses or unity and airy smoothness to
> every flowing pound of the drum.[28]

There are many different forms of traditional drums that have been used by different tribes. Some use the powwow drum, which is a large hide covered wooden framed drum that several people can sit around and drum together as it sits on a stand. Another is the hand drum which is a smaller hide-covered wooden framed drum with hide strings holding everything in place on the back that the drummer uses to hold the drum. This drum can be used sitting, standing, and even moving around if needed. Different drums range in depth and size to meet the desired pitch and sound of the drummer. Another form used by the Comanche is "a small iron kettle covered with animal hide, used to keep song beats during an all-night meeting. The drum contains a handful of stones and a small amount of water."[29] The drum is an iconic part of Native American culture and traditions and has influenced the world of drumming in a myriad of ways. The constant rhythmic sound of the echoing drumbeat stirs the soul and awakens people's spirits.

From a health standpoint drumming has been attributed to reducing chronic pain and trauma, boosting the immune system, stress and anxiety relief, brain rehabilitation, facilitating healthy self-awareness, and promoting connections both within and

28. Garrett and Wilbur, "Does the Worm Live," 194.
29. "Peyote Church."

outward. Ghislaine Goudreau writes, "The participants also discussed the importance of being physically able to use their voices; many Aboriginal women learned to sing when they became involved in hand drumming circles. Overall, participants believed that the beat of the drum is good for their health. Some participants indicated that they gain physical energy from partaking in hand-drumming circles."[30] Rosie Perkins, Sara Ascenso, Louise Atkins, Daisy Fancourt, and Aaron Williamon conclude that "the findings provide support for the conceptual notion of 'creative practice as mutual recovery,' demonstrating that group drumming provides a creative and mutual learning space in which mental health recovery can take place."[31] Lisa Wood, Penny Ivery, Robert Donovan, and Esté E. Lambin approach this from an adolescence view, saying,

> Drumming is an art form with a long history and cross-cultural heritage, and there is a small but growing evidence-base relating to its mental health and wellbeing benefits. Drum circles have been used as a healing ritual in many cultures worldwide for years, and drumming is being increasingly used as a contemporary therapeutic strategy. . . .
>
> . . . Drumming has been described by participants as having a calming influence and it has been associated with stress reduction. In addition, drumming is said to simply make individuals feel good and can help people feel they "fit in" without bearing the stigma of more overt counseling or therapy. Emerging research into the neural development of adolescents suggests innovative interventions that couple physical involvement (e.g. drumming) with other cognitive and behavioral elements can help to bring together experience and emotions that can create strong neural pathway connections.[32]

The power of drumming is a direct way to connect with both God and others. From drumming in the car, at home, using a

30. Goudreau, "Hand Drumming," 76.

31. Perkins et al., "Making Music for Mental Health," 1.

32. Wood et al., "To the Beat," 71.

hand drum, djembe, drum set, or joining on a drum circle, let the rhythms of God blanket your soul and a life of constant drumming with God commence.

COOKING

Cooking has been a staple tradition for many cultures as long as humankind has been mixing ingredients together to delight the palate. Not only is good food beneficial both spiritually and healthwise, but the very act of cooking sacred meals that bring back memories and emotional connections is holy and good. Additionally, cooking leads to eating, which studies and biblical evidence have shown is both a means of grace in people's lives and one of the healthiest activities that can take place. In the Chickasaw tradition we have *pishofa,* also spelled *pashofa.* Traditionally *pashofa* is a rather simple dish cooked in large pots made with Indian corn and pork. "Knowledge of *pishofa* has been shared through oral tradition. Though the healing ceremony is no longer performed, *pishofa* is still an important part of Chickasaw life. *Pishofa* is our national dish, an important symbol of our past. In many cases, iron *pashofa* cooking pots are passed down from generation to generation as family heirlooms. . . . Today we prepare and eat *pishofa* at important gatherings."[33] Traditionally *pashofa* has been affiliated with healing and was a dish accompanied by prayers, singing, and all-night dancing as a way of healing whatever sickness ailed the person.

Another widely known and acclaimed Indian food staple is fry bread. This light bread that is cooked in oil has more variations of recipes per family and tribe than imaginable. It can be served alongside stew, soups, or other dishes as well as covered in honey as a dessert. The most common expression of fry bread is the Indian, or sometimes Navajo, taco. The fry bread, in this case, is piled high with meat, lettuce, tomatoes, salsa, sour cream, and cheese to various degrees and tastes. Kent Nerburn shares, "In

33. "How Do We Know . . ."

Indian country, the sharing of food carries spiritual significance because it is an act of generosity, and generosity is among the most sacred Native values. It harks back to the time in the Native past when a successful harvest or hunt was a cause for sharing and celebration."[34] Nicole Farmer, Katherine Touchton-Leonard, and Alyson Ross suggest that "particularly in the fields of occupational and rehabilitation therapy, research on cooking interventions has focused on cooking as a tool for cognitive and physical evaluation and development. Cooking is used because it is a familiar task of daily living, uses physical engagement, and involves executive function utilization."[35] Julie M. Parsons comes out with a similar conclusion regarding cooking with criminal offenders that the benefits of in-person cooking and eating together show remarkably positive effects for overall health and well-being measured in improved social skills, cultural competencies, and effective relocation back into society.[36]

The act of cooking can be a spiritual practice that awakens the soul to new depths of living with God in unimaginable ways. The sacred act of putting ingredients together in the right amounts and in the right timing using the right methods is a sacred art of survival that dates to the first humans. Like so many Native Americans who carry on the traditions of cooking their sacred meals, explore more deeply what traditional and sacred meals your culture holds. For many, cooking is seen as a daily requirement or chore rather than a spiritual outlet. If cooking is a daily requirement for you in some way, explore what it means to simply "be" instead of to "do" and how cooking on the Indian Road can lead you to finding God.

NATURE

Connection with nature and creation is as Native American as drums, dancing, and fry bread. Native American pantheistic

---

34. Nerburn, *Wisdom of the Native Americans*, 28.

35. Farmer et al., "Psychosocial Benefits of Cooking Interventions," 168.

36. Parsons, "Cooking with Offenders," 8.

beliefs have dominated pop-culture in often misunderstood and sometimes accurate ways. That aside, the deep love and reverence Native American people have held for nature over the centuries is unmatched. The Chickasaw nation approaches this saying, "We cannot separate *yammi ikbitok* (nature) from our spirituality. Natural elements—fire, wood, plants, water, earth, stone, food, sky—were essential to our way of life. Nature gave us the means to make everything we needed in our daily lives: shelters, canoes, baskets and mats, weapons and tools, utensils and cookware and clothing."[37] Cynthia Snavely writes on the importance of grasping the understanding of "spiritual teachings of earth-centered traditions which celebrate the sacred circle of life and instruct us to live in harmony with the rhythms of nature."[38] Bobby Lake-Thom emphasizes this point from a historical view:

> When the first Europeans came to this country, they saw our Native American people praying to the Sun, Moon, Stars, Rivers, and Lakes; to the Trees and Plants; to the Wind, Lightening, and Thunder; and even to Plants, to the Animals, Fish, Snakes, and Rocks. They called us pagans, heathens, and savages. For some strange reason they developed the idea that we did not believe in God, although in many different tribal languages there were references to a Great Spirit, the Great Creator, the Maker, the Great Mystery, or the Great Invisible One. The truth is that not only did the American Indians worship God, but they also respected and communicated with that which God had created.[39]

Rainbow Eagle, Choctaw, centers on five spiritual gifts that Mother Earth offers as the following: a deep appreciation for the gifts around us, a way of spiritual balance, a sense of time and cyclical patterns, a sense of relation to all things, and a deep responsibility with the power we bear. "Native American Spirituality dwells within the words and deeds of honor, respect and love. It

37. "Unbreakable Bond."
38. Snavely, "Native American Spirituality," 92.
39. Lake-Thom, *Spirits of the Earth*, 7.

calls humanity to be a relative to the natural that surrounds our every moment and breath of life."[40] This deeply rooted respect and love for nature and all that is Mother Earth is as central to Native American spirituality as anything else. To find God on the Indian Road of nature is to see God in all things and see all things as having sacred value and worth.

Adele Ahlberg Calhoun writes that the ancient practice of *visio divina* is the practice of intentionally seeking God through praying with images, icons, created media, and creation itself.[41] There are many ways to connect with nature in a spiritual way. A way of "being" that lives into the Native American way of spirituality is a way that honors nature in all places, times, and in all ways. Simply step outside and breathe in the goodness of fresh air that reminds you of the sacredness all around us in creation. Taking pause in these moments of connecting with nature to say thanks, appreciate, and honor are crucial to the spiritual aspects involved. Any time spent in nature should be a holy and spiritual experience that draws us closer to God. Whether daily walking outside, opening the windows when the weather is fair, camping, hiking, fishing, gardening, or any of the other myriad of ways to connect with nature are avenues for spiritual living. Another way is to help Mother Nature; highways and clustered cities are congested with trash and waste selfishly and thoughtlessly thrown out that do extreme harm to our planet's delicate ecosystem. Finding ways for energy efficiency in your home and everyday life can help sustain our planet in ways that will benefit generations after us. Appreciating nature is often overlooked and we take advantage of the wonderful creation around us in so many ways. Sitting on a cool spring day with the rays of sunshine wrapping around you or on a fall day walking through the leaves all bundled up are times to give thanks and appreciate all that God has provided in and through Mother Nature. Instead of "doing" a good act of planting a tree on Arbor Day or Earth Day, let every day be Earth Day as we care for creation so lovingly provided.

40. Eagle, *Walk In the Woods,* 339.
41. Calhoun, *Spiritual Disciplines Handbook,* 46.

SACRED TIME

A Native American sense of time is a concept that can be overlooked in the larger practices of Indian people. Often so many people get caught up on drums, dances, songs, and other more prominent expressions that the understanding of time in Indigenous communities can be easily unnoticed. "American Indians have generally viewed life as a circle. Both birth and death are part of the circle of life. A person moves through four stages of his or her life: childhood, youth, maturity, old age. In each stage, the individual has a role to play and a contribution to make to the community."[42] One example can be found in the Chickasaw calendar and year. "The Chickasaw year, derived from the moon's cycles, had 13 months. Time was measured by the length of a day, the phase of the moon, and by the changing of the seasons. *Hashi' holhtina'*, (notched stick calendar), was one method we used to keep track of time. We also used bundles to mark the days."[43] Similarly the Kiowa "made the most elaborate examples of Plains Indian pictorial calendars. They recorded both a summer and winter pictorial or 'count' for each calendar year. A forked pole, Sun Dance Lodge, or a tree with leaves indicate summer. A bare tree or pole indicated winter. Originally recorded on hides, the majority of surviving Kiowa calendars are recorded on long canvas rolls and are read left to right, starting with the earliest date recorded."[44] A crucial celebration is that of the winter solstice. The winter solstice marks the beginning of winter and the day with the fewest hours of sunlight for the entire year. This is a time where many tribes celebrate and begin the art and sacred practice of storytelling. For some tribes this was also the beginning of a new calendar year, and a new year meant retelling the traditional ways to be remembered and honored.

The seasons of life are often cause for change and even celebration to some extent. In today's context fall denotes a change

42. "Shell Shakers."
43. "Tracking Time."
44. "Kiowa Pictorial Calendar."

of dress and color schemes as the crisp airs of winter begin to nip and chill. As winter approaches people scurry indoors and there is more intimate contact as we huddle around fireplaces and space heaters. Spring brings about new life and celebrations of accomplishment in graduations and is often a time for cleaning and fresh starts. Summer can be a season of both work and play as the warm sun heats the earth and outdoor activities are treasured. The Christian church also has great influence over the calendar year with liturgical seasons being a major influence in many denominations. There are so many rich heritages to draw upon when it comes to time, and it seems almost every single day is a national holiday or national day for celebrating something. The reality is that every single day is a blessing from the Creator. Native Americans knew, know, and will forever know this truth in powerful ways. To find God on the Indian Road regarding time is to let every single moment of every single day be marked with gratitude for the time available. It is to live every single moment as a way of worship and praise to God. It is to make every second an anthem, every minute a hymn, every hour a liturgy, every day a sermon, every week an affirmation of faith, every month a doxology, every year a prayer for illumination, and a lifetime a life song of praise. It means to move past simply "doing" life and "being" present in every single moment, treating it as the last gift we will ever receive. Let our calendars be marked with thanksgiving and praises full of joyful obedience and unwavering faith in all that we face as we live into being sacred timekeepers instead of simple doers of time as our lives pass us by.

SINGING

The songs of Native American peoples are another unique and vast aspect of Indian life and traditions. The first differential is that these songs are sung in languages that are sometimes extremely similar, but rarely the same. This creates a different dialect, and such different vocal traditions have formed. Tara Browner writes that "most pow-wow songs are strophic and have an interior repetition. In Indians performance terminology, dancers call each strophe a 'round' where singers use the term push-up. 'Push-up' refers to pushing the voice to a higher pitch at the beginning of each new strophe and is descriptive of the physical effort of singing."[45] Mary Ella Russel of the Chickasaw tribe shares when speaking of medicine men, "They sang a special song called *Tigbahaka*, and it caused the sick person to get well in a little while, usually. Most people don't know the song anymore. My dad used to sing it."[46] The tradition of singing has been rooted in Native American way of life from our earliest ancestors and has brought spiritual and physical health. The same aspects offered to those seeking a deeper spiritual way of living in harmony and connection with the Creator.

Scientifically speaking, the effects of singing are numerous. "The main finding with respect to endocrine responses is that singing leads to significant positive increases of mean levels of sIgA, which is considered as the first line of defense against infections in the upper respiratory system."[47] "Singing and music making is indicated as a protective factor for cognitive decline. Making music at least once every 2 weeks and especially playing a musical instrument is associated with better attention, episodic memory and executive functions."[48] The act of singing is one that is easy to accomplish in today's time. With radio, online music, portable music devices, Bluetooth headphones, and so many more options, the music world is more easily accessible than ever. Private singing can literally take place at any time in any place. Even online musical collaboration has seen electronic advantages as online collaboration methods, Zoom, live streaming, and other possibilities have made an online musical interaction feasible. Where singing can take place both privately and corporately in so many ways and through so many different avenues, the choices are truly limitless. A life of singing is one that embraces the music of life and allows the music of the soul to live and flourish in everyday ways. "Being"

---

45. Browner, *Heartbeat of the People*, 75.

46. Milligan, *Indian Way: Chickasaws*, 63.

47. Kreutz et al., "Does Singing Provide," 218.

48. Moss et al., *Exploring the Perceived Health Benefits*, 160.

as a way of spiritual living through singing is a life that embraces music in and of all places and is readily available to harmonize with the ups and downs of life.

SWEATS

The Indian sweat lodge is an intertribal practice that has been observed for years for many different reasons and benefits. Spiritual in every way, the sweat lodge has been a place of visioning, purification, and even healing. "Other rituals and practices helped cleanse us. *Hoyahno* (sweats) were a traditional way to drive out contamination. We prayed and shared a pipe as we gathered around the high heat that opened our pores, clearing our mind, spirits and bodies."[49] Joseph Bruchac writes that "two basic types of sweat baths were in common use in North America at the time of the coming of the first Europeans. The vapor-bath sweat involves heating stones in a fire outside the lodge. The stones are carried inside, the lodge is sealed, and after cedar and sweetgrass are placed on the stones, water is poured to create steam."[50] Mr. Bruchac makes the distinct connection between sweat lodges and European steam baths at the time.[51] He also notes, "Because the sweat lodge is so often described as a womb and because the experience of leaving the lodge is often equated with being reborn, it is clear why sweat ledges seem to be universally linked to stories and ideas of creation."[52] Richard Twiss shares the story of several men going through their first sweat together where one man said, "Though it doesn't fit any of my Christian categories either, anything that our people did as a positive influence to our culture and our family was positive in the eyes of Jesus."[53]

49. "Purifying Way."
50. Bruchac, *Native American Sweat Lodge*, 11.
51. Bruchac, *Native American Sweat Lodge*, 15.
52. Bruchac, *Native American Sweat Lodge*, 46.
53. Twiss, *Rescuing the Gospel*, 111.

The suggestion is not to engage in Native American sweat lodge practices, as these are sacred practices to Indian people, but in the spirit of this Native spiritual practice there are contemporary options. Saunas and sweat bathes have been around since Roman and Greek times and have been used in the same spirit as Native Americans have used them for purification and cleansing means. Vandana V. Shiralkar, Pratap E. Jagtap, Gajanan J. Belwalkar, Nitin S. Nagane, and Sushama P. Dhonde conclude that "steam sauna activates many biological systems in the body including the endocrine system. Majority of research on the influence of steam bath on volunteers using steam sauna showed that hyperthermia causes a shift of metabolism toward carbohydrate changes. Steam sauna is an important modality in biological regeneration and is used by athletes and people who do not practice any exercise."[54] Whether it be in a local sauna, steam room, or simply using an at home shower, the health and spiritual benefits of regular steaming are clear. Finding God in the steam as the body is cleansed of impurities is a deeply spiritual act full of opportunities to pray and communicate with God the Creator in powerful ways. The regular and disciplined practice of steaming allows for the Holy Spirit to move more deeply and draw the practitioner into a deeper sense of spiritual awareness and closeness. Finding God on the Indian Road in the steam of saunas and sweat baths is a way to live into this Native Spirit that seeks a deeply spiritual connection with God in times of great joy and hardship.

STICKBALL

It wouldn't be a Native American thing without mentioning the great sport of Native tribes, *itti' kapochcha to'li'*—stickball. Agnes Wallace of the Mississippi Choctaw shared, "Despite the constant threats, our brothers and sisters in the Southeast preserved their way of life. They continued speaking our language, dancing

---

54. Shiralker et al., "Effect of Steam Sauna Bath," 19.

our ancestors' dances, and playing our ancient games, such as stickball."[55] Similar to lacrosse, stickball is played on a circular playing field with a high pole in the center for making goals. Stickball is played on a football-like field, with two poles a hundred yards apart for making goals. An equal number of people per team hurl a ball made of deer hide around a smoothed rock. Players take turns lobbing the ball down the field with ball sticks approximately two feet long, with a rounded end, like the palm of a hand, weaved with deer skin. Players use stickball sticks to hurl the ball down the field to teammates, who then hit or touch the pole to score points. The game can be gruesome at times and is physically and mentally taxing in all regards. Often these matches would be social matches within tribes including men and women, or a means of resolving disputes between tribes where all men teams would typically play.

Like any sport, the health and spiritual advantages are easily noticeable. Jim Parry, Simon Robinson, Nick J. Watson, and Mark Nesti all argue that the spiritual and physical connections to active sport involvement are too numerous to ignore. The authors move that sports often focus on the immense achievements of athletes, neglect to acknowledge the fact beyond great physical feats, and lose sight of the deeply spiritual aspects involved.[56] Rochelle M. Eime, Janet A. Young, Jack T. Harvey, Melanie J. Charity, and Warren R. Payne resolve,

> There is substantive evidence of many different psychological and social health benefits of participation in sport by children and adolescents. Furthermore, there is a general consensus that participation in sport for children and adolescence is associated with improved psychological and social health, above and beyond other forms of leisure-time. More specifically, there are reports that participation in team sports rather than individual activities is associated with better health. It is conjectured that this is due to the social nature of team sport, and that the

55. "Our Traditional Ways."

56. Parry et al., *Sport and Spirituality*, 3.

health benefits are enhanced through positive involvement of peers and adults.[57]

The ancient art of playing stickball in Indigenous communities is not only a means of political and social ends, but also both a physical way of staying healthy and fit and spiritually strong as the warrior ways of tribes can be lived into in the twenty-first century. This sacred way is a testament to the need for physical health in our lives that draws us into a deeper spiritual life as well. In today's world where golf, flag football, tennis, frisbee golf, lacrosse, and so many other communities involving athletic functions are happening, the ways of living a spiritually and physically fit life are infinite. To be a person of great health spiritually and physically is to look at all opportunities of life to be healthy and fit. These actions become much more than simple "doing" as a lifestyle develops of healthy eating, regular exercise, and constant development of healthy habits.

BEADING AND CRAFTING

Native American crafts and arts have been both a staple of the Indigenous community and the most sought after and misappropriated facet of Indian living. Today cheap knock-off versions of traditionally made artifacts can be found in almost every gas station all over the country, and the high market for "Native" type memorabilia and lifestyle is instantly obtainable. Despite the consumer-based mass distribution of defrauded and stereotypical counterfeits, Native Americans are still making traditional goods honoring the historic arts and crafts of our people. From beading and basket weaving to moccasin and dreamcatcher crafting, the old ways are still being kept by Natives today. Many tribes now have established cultural centers that work to preserve and teach these sacred practices to our people and even to the inquiring public. Although crafted and handmade items should never be sold as Native American by anyone that is not truly Native in order

57. Eime et al., *Systematic Review*, 18.

to protect and preserve the sacredness of these traditional ways, learning and these ways can be a way of both respect and reverence if done through appropriate channels. Even more than this, the spirit of these practices gives way to an entire world of spiritual practices for anyone to live into. "Chickasaws often used *nokhistap inno'chi* (special necklaces) to bring prosperity or provide protection. Hunters carried the foot of a dear to help kill more deer, buffalo, beaver, and other animals. Chickasaw women might wear a string of beaded buffalo hair around the legs to ward of such things as miscarriage and hard labor."

BEADING[58]

It's also crucial to note this:

> Beading is a tradition Choctaw people have carried forward over many generations. Even though the types of beads and patterns have changed over the years, a strong value and meaning is still associated with the beauty of beadwork and the intense labor involved in its creation. Traditionally, Choctaw women were the primary beadworkers. They created masterful works that depicted images from Choctaw life and philosophy. Some of the

58. "Beads."

most traditional patterns found in Choctaw beadwork are diamond, representing the Eastern Diamond-Back RattleSnake, or the starburst referencing the Creator in the heavens above. Today you will see both men and women carrying the tradition of beading forward to the next generation. Many patterns, colors, and meanings are attributed to contemporary beadwork. Designs are as unique as the individual make and often reflect personal tastes and values. However, the link to the past is still felt and honored with every creation.[59]

The art and craft of making the beads is extremely difficult and rigorous and took great time and patience. Within the Christian church the deep and rich history of beads is profound. In her book *Beads of Healing: Prayer, Trauma, and Spiritual Wholeness,* Kristen E. Vincent shares how prayer beads allowed her to find a depth spiritually she never thought possible in the wake of the great trauma and grief she suffered at a time in her life. In her devotional she writes, "Prayer beads are tools for prayer. Just as a hammer and nails help us construct a house, so prayer beads help us construct a life of connection with God. The beads are not the end: they are the means to an end, which is communion with God."[60] Whether Roman Catholic and using the Rosary or Protestant and using Prayer Beads, the act of using beads to organize, deepen, and strengthen prayer with God is as ancient as any. Prayer beads offer a way deeper than simply "doing" bead praying when life is difficult or it is convenient, but they offer us the gift of constant prayer and a way of "being" that places us in connection with the Creator in profound and deep ways.

These are just a few of the many practices that can come out of a Native American spirituality when connected with a Christian spirituality of living deeply with God. These examples reveal prime aspects of an entire commitment to spiritual living that involves a profound sense of "being" over simple "doing." There are also many common ways that are shared widely within Native

59. "Today's Beading."
60. Vincent, *Bead and a Prayer,* 16.

American tribes across the US, especially the southeastern tribes located in present day Oklahoma. Deeper study and learning of traditional Native American ways can lead to more expressions of spiritual living at the intersection of traditional Indian ways and Christian spiritual ways.

Conclusion

So back to Ted and that experience in my office that I will never forget. What I learned from that experience was life changing and has brought about a way of living spiritually never imagined. To some in the Native American community, this way of living may seem out of place or inappropriate; drawing upon the centuries of harm and being told to be Christian is to denounce Native practices in their entirety. To the non-Native community, this way of spiritual living in between the worlds of being Indian and Christian may seem foreign and unnatural in its lack purity of and separation. To both communities I invite a new way of thinking and healing to take place. It is high time the hurtful past and voices of hate, oppression, marginalization, and stereotypical nuances fade from existence as Indigenous people begin to find hope and comfort in the fact that traditional spiritual ways of our people were, are, and will forever be just as spiritual as any orthodox or traditional Christian practices. The historic past between early colonists, missionaries, Europeans, and the Indigenous peoples of North America should no longer bear influence on the future outside of its cautionary tone of history repeating itself. The lies, schemes, massacres, thefts, and oppressions of the past are scars that are not yet healed and will never be forgotten by Indian people, but no longer can we let the voices of the past hinder us from finding God on the Indian Road. The misappropriation and stolen ways throughout history lend deeply to the sacredness of the work that is this journeying on the Indian Road as humanness is seen in all persons because all persons are of sacred worth in the eyes of the Great Creator. When Native people can be seen as human, then the spiritual way of living that is inherent to who we are can be shared with all those that bask in the sun of the Creator. When Native people can be seen as human, a mindset can emerge that opens limitless opportunities in communing with God. The spiritual longing to live in deep and constant communion with the Creator of All Things is a longing no culture or person is immune to, and all share in holy ways of how to live into this calling and longing. This longing gives way to the sacred, the holy, the divine to commune with us in profound ways and for a way of living to take place that draws God into every aspect. A new way of finding God on the Indian Road is emerging that centers on a deep sense of "being" instead of surface level "doing," and it is when, and if, the Christian church can begin to appreciate, respect, and revere the Native American people and Native ways of life that a new path to spiritual living with God can arise. The spiritual growth needed today is one of authenticity and deep faith that treasures the ways of the past while finding respect and reverence in hearing the sacred voices of an Indigenous people who have so much to offer. The ways of old will become the ways of new as Native American spiritual traditions offer a new way forward in spiritual living and a possible new age for the church to embrace and commence. From Pashofa pots and stickball courses to powwow dances and the reverberating drums, the Native American spiritual way offers a new and fresh way of living in communion with God. Ultimately the Indian Road is long and winding, holding more treasures than imaginable along its windings and turns. For centuries Natives have found God on this road in ways some can only imagine. Ways full of mystery that sound outlandish or even mythical but have guided a people to the Creator for centuries. Finding God on the Indian Road is less of a challenge of hide-and-seek and more of a challenge of how long will you stay on the road walking with God? As a great Shoshone Elder once said, "Do not begrudge the white man his presence on this land. Though he doesn't know it yet, he has come here to learn from us."[1] The way of the Native, the way of

---

1. Nerburn, *Wisdom of the Native Americans*, 28.

the Indian Road, is a path some will never follow, but for those that do venture along this path, God is there waiting to be found. May we greet the Creator joyfully on the Indian Road saying, "Though I walk in moccasins, my footsteps follow thee."[2]

2. Testerman, *Footprints Still Whispering*, 12.

Bibliography

"600 Generations." Wall text, Heritage Gallery. Choctaw Cultural Center, Calera, OK.

"AD 1493: The Pope Asserts Rights to Colonize, Convert, and Enslave." National Library of Medicine. https://www.nlm.nih.gov/nativevoices/timeline/171.html.

Adair, James. *The History of the American Indians*. Tuscaloosa, AL: University of Alabama Press, 2017.

"Adeline Hudson." Wall text, Choctaw People. Choctaw Cultural Center, Calera, OK.

Aldred, Lisa. "Plastic Shamans and Astroturf Sun Dances: New Age Commercialism of Native American Spirituality." *American Indian Quarterly* 24.3 (2000) 597–614.

Alfred, Taiaiake, and Jess Corntassel. "Being Indigenous: Resurgences against Contemporary Colonialism." *Politics of Identity* 9 (2005) 597.

Alpert, Patricia T. "The Health Benefits of Dance." *Home Health Care Management & Practice* 23.2 (2011) 155–57.

Ang, Daniel. "Diminishing Mass Attendance: A Pressing Ecclesial Concern." *Compass: A Review of Topical Theology* 42.3 (Spring 2008) 21–24.

"Beads." Wall text, Heritage Gallery. Chickasaw Cultural Center, Sulphur, OK.

Berny, Martin. "The Hollywood Indian Stereotype: The Cinematic Othering and Assimilation of Native Americans at the Turn of the 20th Century." *Angles: New Perspectives on the Anglophone World* 10 (2020) 1–53.

Bevins, Winfield. *Ever Ancient, Ever New: The Allure of Liturgy for a New Generation*. Grand Rapids: Winfield Bevins, 2019.

"Blood of the Ground." Wall text, Heritage Exhibit. Washita Battlefield National Historic Site, Cheyenne, OK.

Bonhoeffer, Dietrich. *The Cost of Discipleship*. Chicago: Touchstone, 1995.

———. *Spiritual Care*. Philadelphia: Fortress Press, 1985.

Boyd, Julia. "An Examination of Native Americans in Film and Rise of Native Filmmakers." *The Elon Journal of Undergraduate Research in Communications* 6.1 (Spring 2015) 105–13. https://eloncdn.blob.core.windows.net/eu3/sites/153/2017/06/10BoydEJSpring15.pdf.

Brill, Charles J. *Custer, Black Kettle, and the Fight on the Washita*. Norman, OK: Oklahoma University Press, 2002.

"Broken Promises." Wall display, Heritage Exhibit. Chickasaw Cultural Center, Sulphur City, OK.

Browner, Tara. *Heartbeat of the People: Music and Dance of the Northern Powwow*. Chicago: University of Illinois, 2004.

Brown, Joseph Epes. *The Spiritual Legacy of the American Indian*. Bloomington, IN: World Wisdom, 2007.

Bruchac, Joseph. *The Native American Sweat Lodge: History and Legends*. Freedom, CA: Crossing, 1993.

"Buffalo People." Wall text, Heritage Exhibit. Comanche National Museum and Cultural Center, Lawton, OK.

"Buffalo." Wall text, Heritage Exhibit. Comanche National Museum and Cultural Center, Lawton, OK.

Calhoun, Adele Ahlberg. *Spiritual Disciplines Handbook: Practices That Transform Us*. Downers Grove: InterVarsity, 2015.

"The Cheyenne and Arapaho Tribes of Oklahoma." Wall text, Heritage Exhibit. Washita Battlefield National Historic Site, Cheyenne, OK.

"Cheyenne Leadership." Wall text, Heritage Gallery. Cheyenne Cultural Center, Clinton, OK.

"Chicashsha chiyama chikanoma." Wall display, Heritage Exhibit. Chickasaw Cultural Center, Sulphur City, OK.

"Chickasaw Lineage." Wall text, Tribes of Oklahoma. Five Civilized Tribes Museum, Muskogee, OK.

"Chickasaw Nation." Wall text, Tribes of Oklahoma. Five Civilized Tribes Museum, Muskogee, OK.

"Chickashsha alhiha ittafamma." Wall text, Native American Heritage Gallery. Oklahoma History Center, Oklahoma City.

"The Choctaw People." Wall Display, Our People. Choctaw Cultural Center, Calera, OK.

"Comanche Children." Wall text, Heritage Exhibit. Comanche National Museum and Cultural Center, Lawton, OK.

Clark, Blue. *Indian Tribes of Oklahoma: A Guide*. Norman, OK: Oklahoma University Press, 2009.

Cobb, Amanda J., and Linda Hogan. *Chickasaw: Unconquered and Unconquerable*. Portland: Graphic Arts, 2006.

Columbus, Christopher. "The Letter of Columbus to Luis De Sant Angel Announcing His Discovery." US History, 1995. https://www.ushistory.org/documents/columbus.htm.

"Comanche Women." Wall text, Heritage Exhibit. Comanche National Museum and Cultural Center, Lawton, OK.

"Compilation of Everyday Scenes from Yellow Nose Ledger Art." Wall text, Heritage Exhibit. Washita Battlefield National Historic Site, Cheyenne, OK.

"Cooking Month." Wall text, Heritage Gallery. Choctaw Cultural Center, Calera, OK.

Currier, Charles Warren. *History of Religious Orders: Together with a Brief History of the Catholic Church in Relation to Religious Orders.* Sheridan, WY: Creative Media Partners, 2015.

Curtice, Kaitlin B. *Native: Identity, Belonging, and Rediscovering God.* Grand Rapids: Brazos, 2020.

"Dances." Wall display, Heritage Exhibit. Washita Battlefield National Historic Site, Cheyenne, OK.

"Deadly First Encounter." Wall text, Heritage Gallery. Chickasaw Cultural Center, Sulphur, OK.

Deloria, Vine, Jr., and David E. Wilkins. *Tribes, Treaties, and Constitutional Tribulations.* Austin: University of Texas Press, 1999.

Downey, David. "After Riverside Teacher's Mock Native American Chant, Officials Announce Plan." *The Press-Enterprise,* Nov 9, 2021. https://www.pe.com/2021/11/08/after-riverside-teachers-mock-native-american-chant-officials-announce-plan/.

Eagle, Rainbow. *A Walk in the Woods.* Zanesfield, OH: Rainbow Light, 2016.

"Early Life." Wall text, Heritage Exhibit. Comanche National Museum and Cultural Center, Lawton, OK.

Echo-Hawk, Walter R. *In the Courts of the Conqueror: The 10 Worst Indian Law Cases Ever Decided.* Golden, CO: Fulcrum, 2010.

Eime, Rochelle M., et al. "A Systematic Review of the Psychological and Social Benefits of Participation in Sport for Children and Adolescents: Informing Development of a Conceptual Model of Health through Sport." *International Journal of Behavioral Nutrition and Physical Activity* 10.98 (2013) 2-21.

"European Encounters." Wall text, Heritage Gallery. Chickasaw Cultural Center, Sulphur, OK.

Farmer, Nicole, et al. "Psychosocial Benefits of Cooking Interventions: A Systematic Review." *Health Education & Behavior* 45.2 (2018) 167–80.

Fisher, Linford D. *The Indian Great Awakening: Religion and the Shaping of Native Cultures in Early America.* New York: Oxford University Press, 2012.

"Fish Killing." Wall text, Native American Heritage Gallery. Oklahoma History Center, Oklahoma City.

"The Five CIVILIZED Tribes." Wall text, The Term Civilized. Five Civilized Tribes Museum, Muscogee, OK.

"Food Sources." Wall text, Heritage Exhibit. Comanche National Museum and Cultural Center, Lawton, OK.

Garoutte, Eva Marie, et al. "Spirituality and Attempted Suicide among American Indians." *Social Science and Medicine* 56 (2003) 1571-1579.

Garrett, Michael Tlanastu, and Michael P. Wilbur. "Does the Worm Live in the Ground? Reflections on Native American Spirituality." *Journal of Multicultural Counseling and Development* 27.4 (2011) 193-206.

Goodfeather, Doug. *Think Indigenous: Native American Spirituality for a Modern World*. Carlsbad, CA: Hay House, 2021.

Goudreau, Ghislaine. "Hand Drumming: Health-Promoting Experiences of Aboriginal Women from a Northern Ontario Urban Community." *Journal de la Santé Autochtone* 4.1 (2008) 72–83.

"The Green Corn Ceremony." Wall text, Native American Heritage Gallery. Oklahoma History Center, Oklahoma City.

Hahn, Heather. "The Making of Thanksgiving in the US." UM News, Nov 19, 2020. https://www.umnews.org/en/news/the-making-of-thanksgiving-in-the-us.

Harjo, Suzan Shown. *Nation to Nation: Treatise Between the United States and American Indian Nations*. Washington, DC: Smithsonian Institute, 2014.

Heath, Elaine. *Five Means of Grace: Experiencing God's Love the Wesleyan Way*. Nashville: Abingdon, 2017.

HeavyRunner, Iris, and Joann Sebastian Morris. "Traditional Native Culture and Resilience." The University of Minnesota Digital Conservancy, 1997. https://hdl.handle.net/11299/145989.

"The Heartbeat of a Nation." Chickasaw Cultural Center, 2022. https://web.archive.org/web/20220117043935/https://chickasawculturalcenter.com/about-us.

Hernández-Ávila, Inés. "Mediations of the Spirit: Native American Religious Traditions and the Ethics of Representation." *American Indian Quarterly* 20.3 (Summer–Autumn 1996) 329–352.

"Historic Tribes: Ponca." Outdoor display. Standing Bear Museum and Education Center, Ponca City, OK.

Hodge, David R., and Gordon E. Limb. "A Native American Perspective on Spiritual Assessment: The Strengths and Limitations of a Complementary Set of Assessment Tools." *Health & Social Work* 35.2 (2010) 121–31.

Holder, Arthur. *The Blackwell Companion to Christian Spirituality*. Malden, MA: Blackwell, 2005.

"A Horse People." Wall text, Heritage Exhibit. Comanche National Museum and Cultural Center, Lawton, OK.

Houtman, Dick, and Stef Aupers. "The Spiritual Turn and the Decline of Tradition: The Spread of Post-Christian Spirituality in 14 Western Countries." *Journal for the Scientific Study of Religion* 46.3 (2007) 305–20.

Howard, Evan B. *A Guide to Christian Spiritual Formation: How Scripture, Spirit, Community, and Mission Shape Our Souls*. Grand Rapids: Baker Academic, 2018.

"How Do We Know . . ." Wall text, Heritage Gallery. Chickasaw Cultural Center, Sulphur, OK.

Hoxie, Frederick E., ed. *The Oxford Handbook of American Indian History*. New York: Oxford University Press, 2016.

Irwin, Lee. "Themes in Native American Spirituality." *American Indian Quarterly* 21.1 (1996) 309–26.

"Jerry Lowman." Wall text, Heritage Gallery. Choctaw Cultural Center, Calera, OK.

Johansen, Bruce E., ed. *Enduring Legacies: Native American Treaties and Contemporary Controversies*. Westport, CT: Praeger, 2004.

Keogh, Justin W. L., et al. "Physical Benefits of Dancing for Healthy Older Adults: A Review." *Journal of Aging and Physical Activity* 17 (2009) 479–500.

Kimmerer, Robin Wall. *Braiding Sweetgrass: Indigenous Wisdom, Scientific Knowledge, and the Teaching of Plants*. Minneapolis, MN: Milkweed Editions, 2013.

King, Martin Luther, Jr. "Rediscovering Lost Values." The Martin Luther King, Jr. Research and Education Institute, Feb 28, 1954. https://kinginstitute.stanford.edu/king-papers/documents/rediscovering-lost-values-0.

"Kiowa Pictorial Calendar." Wall text, Heritage Gallery. Oklahoma History Center, Oklahoma City.

Kohn, Margaret, and Kavita Reddy. "Colonialism." The Stanford Encyclopedia of Philosophy Archive, edited by Edward N. Zalta, Aug 29, 2017. https://plato.stanford.edu/archives/fall2017/entries/colonialism/.

Kreutz, Gunter, et al. "Does Singing Provide Health Benefits?" *Journal of Behavioral Medicine* 27.6 (Jan 2005) 623–35.

Lake-Thom, Bobby. *Spirits of the Earth*. New York: Penguin, 1997.

"Language." Wall text, Native American Heritage Gallery. Oklahoma History Center, Oklahoma City.

Levison, Jack. *40 Days with the Holy Spirit*. Brewster, MA: Paraclete, 2015.

"Life Lesson." Wall text, Heritage Gallery. Chickasaw Cultural Center, Sulphur, OK.

Linn, Denise. *Kindling the Native Spirit: Sacred Practices for Everyday Life*. Carlsbad, CA: Hay, 2015.

"Loski' chalha'chi.'" Wall text, Heritage Gallery. Chickasaw Cultural Center, Sulphur, OK.

Lowney, Chris. *Pope Francis: Why He Leads the Way He Leads*. Chicago: Loyola, 2013.

Mann, Charles C. *1491: New Revelations of the Americas before Columbus*. New York: Vintage, 2005.

———. *1493: Uncovering the New World Columbus Created*. New York: Vintage, 2011.

Mann, Henrietta, and Anita Phillips. *On This Spirit Walk: The Voices of Native American and Indigenous Peoples*. Muskogee, OK: Native American Comprehensive Plan, 2012.

Marshall, Joseph M., III. *The Lakota Way: Stories and Lessons for Living*. New York: Penguin, 2001.

Martin, Joel W., and Mark A. Nicholas. *Native Americans, Christianity, and the Reshaping of the American Religious Landscape*. Chapel Hill, NC: University of North Carolina Press, 2010.

McPhearson, Dennis H., and J. Douglas Rabb. *Indian from the Inside: Native American Philosophy and Cultural Renewal.* Jefferson, NC: McFarland & Co., 2011.

Mele, Domenec, and Joan Fontradona. "Christian Ethics and Spirituality in Leading Business Organizations: Editorial Introduction." *Journal of Business Ethics* 145 (2017) 671–79.

Milligan, Dorothy. *The Indian Way: Chickasaws.* Ada, OK: Chickasaw, 2021.

"Modern Indian Christians." Wall text, Native American Heritage Gallery. Oklahoma History Center, Oklahoma City.

Moss, Hillary, et al. "Exploring the Perceived Health Benefits of Singing in a Choir: An International Cross-Sectional Mixed-Methods Study." *Perspectives in Public Health* 138.3 (2018) 134.

"Mound Building." Wall text, Heritage Gallery. Choctaw Cultural Center, Calera, OK.

"The Na'II'ES Sunrise Ceremony." Wall text, Native American Heritage Gallery. Oklahoma History Center, Oklahoma City.

"Native American Removal from the Southeast." National Geographic Society, 2002. https://www.nationalgeographic.org/photo/indian-removal/.

Neafsey, John. *A Sacred Voice Is Calling: Personal Vocation and Social Conscience.* Maryknoll, NY: Orbis, 2006.

Nelson, James M. *Psychology, Religion, and Spirituality.* New York: Springer, 2009.

Nerburn, Kent. *The Wisdom of the Native Americans.* Navato, CA: Nor World Library, 1999.

"Nunna Momat Chicashsha." Wall text, Native American Heritage Gallery. Oklahoma History Center, Oklahoma City.

"Oklahoma Indians: We Are Who We Were." Video, Native American Heritage Gallery. The Oklahoma History Center, Oklahoma City.

"Our Creation Stories." Wall text, Heritage Gallery. Choctaw Cultural Center, Calera, OK.

"Our Traditional Ways, 3." Wall text, Heritage Exhibit. Choctaw Cultural Center, Calera, OK.

"Outsiders Arrive." Wall text, Heritage Gallery. Chickasaw Cultural Center, Sulphur, OK.

Page, Jake. *In the Hands of the Great Spirit: The 20,000-Year History of American Indians.* New York: Free Press, 2003.

Parry, Jim, et al. *Sport and Spirituality: An Introduction.* New York: Routledge, 2007.

Parsons, Julie M. "Cooking with Offenders to Improve Health and Well-Being." *British Food Journal* 119.5 (May 2017) 1079–90.

Patterson, Jim. "Pastor Reflects on Abuses at Indian Boarding Schools." UM News, Aug 18, 2021. https://www.umnews.org/en/news/pastor-reflects-on-dark-days-at-indian-boarding-schools.

"Peace Chief Black Kettle." Wall text, Heritage Exhibit. Washita Battlefield National Historic Site, Cheyenne, OK.

"People of the Mother Mound." Wall text, Heritage Gallery. Choctaw Cultural Center, Calera, OK.

"The People." Wall text, Heritage Exhibit. Washita Battlefield National Historic Site, Cheyenne, OK.

Perkins, Rosie, et al. "Making Music for Mental Health: How Group Drumming Mediates Recovery." *Psychology of Well-Being* 6.11 (2016) 1–17. https:// psywb.springeropen.com/articles/10.1186/s13612-016-0048-0.

Pevans, Stephen L. *The Rights of Indians and Tribes.* 4th ed. New York: Oxford University Press, 2012.

"Peyote Church." Wall text, Heritage Exhibit. Comanche National Museum and Cultural Center, Lawton, OK.

"Pictorial Calendars." Wall text, Native American Heritage Gallery. Oklahoma History Center, Oklahoma City.

"Preservation of Indian Cultures." Wall text, Native American Heritage Gallery. Oklahoma History Center, Oklahoma City.

"Purifying Way." Wall text, Heritage Gallery. Chickasaw Cultural Center, Sulphur, OK.

Reiser, William. *Seeking God in All Things: Theology and Spiritual Direction.* Collegeville, MN: Order of Saint Benedict, 2004.

Roberts, Gary L. *Massacre at Sand Creek: How Methodists Were Involved in an American Tragedy.* Nashville: Abingdon, 2016.

"Sacred People." Wall text, Heritage Gallery. Chickasaw Cultural Center, Sulphur, OK.

"Henrietta Mann." Wall text, Sand Creek Exhibit. Washita Battlefield National Historic Site, Cheyenne, OK.

"Servant Leadership." Wall text, Choctaw Leadership. Choctaw Cultural Center, Calera, OK.

"Shell Shakers." Wall text, Native American Heritage Gallery. Oklahoma History Center, Oklahoma City.

Shimer, Porter. *Healing Secrets of the Native Americans: Herbs, Remedies, and Practices That Restore the Body, Mind, and Spirit.* New York: Black Dog and Leventhal, 2004.

Shiralker, Vandana V., et al. "Effect of Steam Sauna Bath on Fasting Blood Glucose Level in Healthy Adults." *Indian Journal of Medical Biochemistry* 22.1 (2018) 18–21.

Snavely, Cynthia. "Native American Spirituality." *Journal of Religious & Theological Information* 4.1 (2008) 91–103.

"Spirituality: Community, Harmony, Ceremony." Wall text, Native American Heritage Gallery. Oklahoma History Center, Oklahoma City.

"Standing Bear Monument." Wall text, Walking Trail. Standing Bear Museum and Education Center, Ponca City, OK.

"Still Dancing." Wall text, Native American Heritage Gallery. Oklahoma History Center, Oklahoma City.

"A Suffering People." Wall text, Heritage Exhibit. Washita Battlefield National Historic Site, Cheyenne, OK.

"Taking up the Warpath." Wall text, Native American Heritage Gallery. Oklahoma History Center, Oklahoma City.

Testerman, Margie. *Footprints Still Whispering in the Wind*. 1st ed. Ada, OK: Chickasaw, 2013.

Thompson, Marjories J. *Soul Feast: An Invitation to the Christian Spiritual Life*. Louisville: Westminster, 1995.

"Today's Beading." Wall text, Heritage Center. Five Civilized Tribes Museum, Muscogee, OK.

Torres Stone, Rosalie A., et al. "Traditional Practices, Traditional Spirituality, and Alcohol Cessation among American Indians." *Journal of Studies on Alchohol* 67 (2006) 236–44.

"Tracking Time." Wall text, Heritage Gallery. Chickasaw Cultural Center, Sulphur, OK.

"Traditional Art." Wall text, Heritage Gallery. Choctaw Cultural Center, Calera, OK.

Treat, James. *Native and Christian: Indigenous Voices on Religious Identity in the United States and Canada*. New York: Routledge, 1996.

"Treaty of Dancing Rabbit Creek Stand." Wall text, Treaties. Choctaw Cultural Center, Calera, OK.

"Treaty of Doak's Stand." Wall text, Treaties. Choctaw Cultural Center, Calera, OK.

"Treaty of Mobile Stand." Wall text, Treaties. Choctaw Cultural Center, Calera, OK.

"Tushpa's Story." Wall display, Our People. Choctaw Cultural Center, Calera, OK.

Twiss, Richard. *One Church, Many Tribes: Following Jesus the Way God Made You*. Minneapolis: Chosen, 2000.

———. *Rescuing the Gospel from the Cowboys: A Native American Expression of the Jesus Way*. Downers Grove: InterVarsity, 2015.

"An Unbreakable Bond." Wall text, Heritage Gallery. Chickasaw Cultural Center, Sulphur, OK.

"Uniquely Chickasaw." Wall display, Heritage Exhibit. Chickasaw Cultural Center, Sulphur City, OK.

"Useful Plants." Wall text, Native American Heritage Gallery. Oklahoma History Center, Oklahoma City.

Vincent, Kristen E. *A Bead and a Prayer: A Beginners Guide to Protestant Prayer Beads*. Nashville: Upper Room, 2013.

"Walking Trail." Display text, Museum Exhibit. Standing Bear Museum and Education Center, Ponca City, OK.

"Wall of Misrepresentations." Wall text, Heritage Exhibit. First Americans Museum, Oklahoma City.

Warrior, Robert Allen. "Canaanites, Cowboys, and Indians: Deliverance, Conquest, and Liberation Theology Today." *Christianity Crisis* (Sep 1989) 21–26. https://www.rmselca.org/sites/rmselca.org/files/media/canaanites_cowboys_and_indians.pdf.

"Warrior Spirit." Wall text, Food Sources. Comanche National Museum and Cultural Center, Lawton, OK.

"We Are Chickasaw." Wall display, Heritage Exhibit. Chickasaw Cultural Center, Sulphur City, OK.

Wesley, John. *The Journal of John Wesley*. Edited by Percy L. Parker. Chicago, IL: Moody, 1974.

West, Cornel. *Prophetic Thought in Postmodern Times*. Monroe, ME: Common Courage, 1993.

Willard, Dallas. *The Spirit of the Disciplines: Understanding How God Changes Lives*. New York: HarperCollins, 1991.

Wood, Lisa, et al. "'To the Beat of a Different Drum': Improving the Social and Mental Wellbeing of At-Risk Young People through Drumming." *Journal of Public and Mental Health* 12.2 (2013) 70–79.

"Yammat sishto-at chimmi fannat apachitok." Wall display, Heritage Exhibit. Chickasaw Cultural Center, Sulphur City, OK.

Yellow Bird, Michael. "Cowboys and Indians: Toys of Genocide, Icons of American Colonialism." *Wicazo Sa Review* 19.2 (2004) 33–48.